POCKET GUIDE

BIRDS

OF NAMIBIA

IAN SINCLAIR & JORIS KOMEN

T0352544

To my daughter, Kiera. Ian Sinclair
As always, to Liz. Joris Komen

Published by Struik Nature
(an imprint of Penguin Random House
South Africa (Pty) Ltd)
Reg. No. 1953/000441/07
The Estuaries No. 4, Oxbow Crescent
Century Avenue, Century City, 7441
South Africa

PO Box 1144, Cape Town,
8000 South Africa

Visit **www.penguinrandomhouse.co.za**
and join the Struik Nature Club for updates,
news, events and special offers.

First published in 2017

10 9 8 7 6 5 4 3

ISBN 978 1 77584 522 5
ePub: 978 1 77584 523 2
ePDF: 978 1 77584 524 9

Publisher: Pippa Parker
Managing editor: Helen de Villiers
Editor: Emily Bowles
Designer: Gillian Black
Cartographers: Neil Bester and
Liezel Bohdanowicz
Typesetter: Deirdré Geldenhuys
Proofreader: Thea Grobbelaar

Reproduction by Resolution Colour (Pty)
Ltd., Cape Town
Printed and bound in China by RR Donnelley

Front cover: White-tailed Shrike (G. McGill
www.sabirdingphotography.co.za)
Back cover, top to bottom: Bateleur
(N. Dennis/Images of Africa); Cardinal
Woodpecker (A. Froneman/Images of
Africa); African Spoonbill; Rosy-faced
Lovebird; Swainson's Spurfowl
Page 1: Crimson-breasted Shrike
(A. Froneman/Images of Africa)
Opposite: Rockrunner (P. Ryan)

MIX
Paper from
responsible sources
FSC® C144853

ACKNOWLEDGEMENTS

Our great appreciation and thanks to all the photographers who came to the
rescue and provided images in the hectic last days of production and especially to
Adam Riley and his team at Rockjumper. Maans Booysen went the extra yard to
secure many images especially for this title.

To all our friends in Namibia who welcomed us with warmth and friendship.
Mark & Charlie Paxton at their great lodge at Shamvuru, Kurt Ingo-Sagell at the
excellent Caprivi Houseboat Safaris, the staff at the Erongo Wilderness Lodge
and Hilary at the Kunene River Lodge, Steve, Louise, Dayne and Sean Braine
at Hobatere and beyond, Mark Boorman, John Paterson and Peter Bridgeford
in the coastal wetlands of Namibia, Coleen Mannheimer of Namibia's National
Herbarium, Brian Schmidt of the Smithsonian Institute and staff of the National
Museum of Namibia.

At Penguin Random House, thanks to Pippa Parker and to Emily Donaldson
and Gillian Black for their tireless efforts to get everything just right.

CONTENTS

INTRODUCTION

Namibia is a vast, mostly uninhabited country. The very name conjures up an image of wide, open deserts, endless sand dunes and a coastline edged with the skeletons of wrecked ships. This is true for only a part of the country, however; the remaining area is remarkably diverse, and as such a haven for a variety of birds.

For example, there is the riverine forest of the Zambezi (Caprivi) Region, and west of this narrow strip, endless teak woodlands. The enormous river systems in the north, which drain the eastern Angolan highlands, meet to form the Okavango River, which flows into the permanent papyrus-choked wetlands of the Okavango panhandle, an enigmatic area renowned for its game and birdlife. Further west and south, seasonally flooded pans hold a myriad waterbirds. In particular, the pans of the Etosha National Park are known for the breeding flamingo population, as well as concentrations of Wattled and Blue cranes.

Moist and arid tree-and-shrub savanna extend over northern and central Namibia, interrupted by impressive mountain ranges of the escarpment zone merging into Nama karoo dwarf shrub vegetation, until the desert edge reveals itself in its true starkness. Dry gravel plains give way to mountainous sand dunes and to a foggy coastline sparsely interrupted with bays and estuaries, oases for all kinds of birds.

Offshore is the cold Benguela Current, an oceanic upwelling that provides a food source for huge populations of local seabirds and for visitors from both polar regions.

Namibia is home to some 690 bird species of which 110 species are endemic or near-endemic, that is birds found nowhere else (endemic) or with ranges extending just beyond the region (near-endemic). Some 357 bird species are described in this guide, the selection based on the most common or likely to be seen in the popular tourist areas.

Virtually wherever you are in Namibia you will see birds, and the challenge then arises to identify them correctly. Even the most remote and hostile areas of the Namib Desert contain birds, and an alert observer will soon find larks, coursers and korhaans beautifully camouflaged in the dunes and gravel fields.

Learning to identify birds is a long and slow process and it takes years of experience to develop the skills needed to tell the obscure species from the

Wattled Cranes often feed in swampy areas.

L. MICHLER / IMAGES OF AFRICA

An African Fish Eagle takes flight with prey.

'little brown jobs': herein lies the challenge and the fascination of birding. Most beginners are put off by the enormous variety of shorebirds, seabirds, pipits, warblers and larks. This should not be a consideration in the early stages of birding. First familiarise yourself with the large, more obvious birds. When the identification of the first hundred or more species is accomplished, the rest become easier with time.

HOW TO USE THIS BOOK

This pocket-sized book has been designed primarily for use in the field, but if you peruse it at leisure you will reap further benefits. By studying the photographs frequently you will be able to remember many of the birds. For example, if you have looked at the photograph of the Lilac-breasted Roller many times you will instantly recognise the bird the very first time you encounter it in the field. This applies to many other birds depicted in this guide except for the unremarkable or nondescript species.

The photographs have been chosen to show the birds' most obvious identifying features. Where there is a marked difference – between the sexes, between breeding (br.) and non-breeding (non-br.) plumage, or between adult (ad.), immature (imm.) and juvenile (juv.) – more than one photograph has been included. An up-to-date distribution map accompanies each species entry, giving a sense of where in the region the bird occurs. Each bird is ascribed its English, Afrikaans, German and scientific names. The length (L) of the bird (from bill tip to outstretched tail) is also given, except in the case of the Ostrich where the height (H) is given.

The text is brief and to the point and the *italicised* phrases highlight the diagnostic features; knowing the most obvious field characters of a bird aids quick identification. A knowledge of calls, either learnt in the field or from recordings, is also recommended. The call of a species is, however, only mentioned in the text if it is a distinguishing characteristic of the bird.

Note that the habitat in which a bird is found is often an important clue to its identity; for example, the African Oystercatcher is confined to rocky shore habitats where it can find the molluscs and crustaceans that comprise its main diet. Similarly, the Dune Lark occurs only in a very restricted area among the dunes of the Namib Desert and knowing this will help you to narrow down the field of possibilities considerably.

VEGETATION ZONES OF NAMIBIA

The map that follows shows the major vegetation zones (biomes) found across Namibia. Bird distribution may be contained by, or even restricted to, specialised habitats within these zones; some birds, however, may be widespread across several vegetation zones.

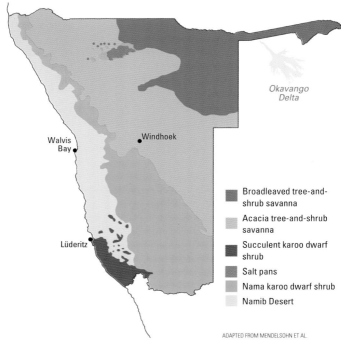

Okavango Delta

Walvis Bay
Windhoek
Lüderitz

- ■ Broadleaved tree-and-shrub savanna
- ■ Acacia tree-and-shrub savanna
- ■ Succulent karoo dwarf shrub
- ■ Salt pans
- ■ Nama karoo dwarf shrub
- ■ Namib Desert

ADAPTED FROM MENDELSOHN ET AL.

Broadleaved tree-and-shrub savanna

The broadleaved tree-and-shrub savanna biome is semi-arid in the west, but receives increasingly more rainfall further east. Growing on deep Kalahari sands, the vegetation is dominated by several species of tall tree, including teak, which form a thick canopy in places. Several large perennial rivers and their floodplains are associated with this biome.

Acacia tree-and-shrub savanna

The semi-arid acacia tree-and-shrub savanna experiences summer rainfall. It is characterised by large expanses of grassland, with a mostly open canopy of thorn trees. The trees are tallest on the deep Kalahari sands in the east, and become more shrubby on the shallower soils and rocky landscapes in the west.

W. BRUENKEN/WIKIMEDIA/CC BY SA 2.5

Succulent karoo dwarf shrub

The landscape of the succulent karoo dwarf shrub biome is harsh, with a pattern of low winter rainfall. It offers a variety of habitats and the great diversity of succulents makes it one of Namibia's most important botanical areas, with many specially protected endemic plants.

BRIAN SCHMIDT

Salt pans

Grasses and dwarf shrubs grow on the plains that surround the Etosha salt pan and other smaller pans in this biome. The area is characterised by saline and limestone soils, which limit the growth of trees. The pans are flooded seasonally, following good rains.

GREG WILLIS/WIKIMEDIA/CC BY SA 3.0

Nama karoo dwarf shrub

This semi-arid biome includes the escarpment zone, which separates the Namib desert from the tree-and-shrub savannas in central and eastern Namibia. Further south, it includes vast plains, pans and mountains with typically low shrub vegetation, grasslands and diverse succulents.

S. WOODHALL

Namib Desert

Characterised by gravel plains, huge sand dunes, rocky hills and mountains, this biome is extremely dry, resulting in very sparse vegetation except for trees and shrubs along the seasonal rivers that cut through to the coast.

C. POUCH/IOA

BEST BIRDING SITES IN NAMIBIA

For a country dominated largely by desert, Namibia is remarkably rich in birding areas. In fact, 21 important birding areas (IBAs) have been recognised, and five Ramsar wetlands -- making it an excellent birding destination.

Among the most popular areas for birding are the Okavango/Zambezi area, Walvis Bay/Namib Desert and the Etosha National Park.

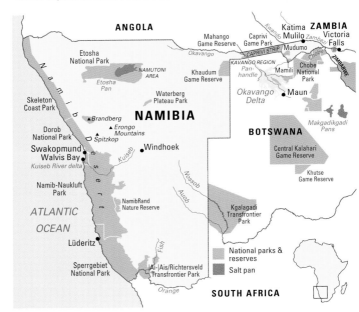

Okavango/Zambezi Region

For travellers venturing to the northeastern reaches of the country, en route to Victoria Falls, the wetlands of the Okavango and Zambezi rivers host some of Namibia's most sought-after bird species.

The Mahango Game Reserve on the Okavango River is one of southern Africa's top birding destinations, with an impressive list of more than 400 bird species. Many of these 'specials' are beyond the scope of this book, but are worth looking out for if you venture to this remote area.

Further east, on the Kwando River in the Zambezi Region, and around

Slaty Egret

Rock Pratincole

African Skimmer

Pygmy Goose

Black Coucal

Katima Mulilo on the Zambezi River, the floodplains, riverine forests and teak woodlands offer a rich spectrum of both wetland and woodland species hard to find elsewhere in southern Africa. They include Bradfield's Hornbill, Black and Coppery-tailed coucals, Pygmy Goose, Coqui Francolin, Lesser Moorhen, Allen's Gallinule, Long-toed Plover, Meyer's Parrot and Schalow's Turaco.

On the Botswanan side, across the border, the Okavango Delta's Panhandle is home to wetland species such as Slaty Egret, African Skimmer, Rock Pratincole, Hartlaub's Babbler, Swamp Boubou, Chirping and Luapula cisticolas. Few people realise that these signature wetland species are easily seen in the wetlands of the Okavango and Zambezi, on good all-season roads.

Long-toed Plover

Meyer's Parrot

Lesser Flamingoes

Damara Tern

Benguela Long-billed Lark

Namaqua Sandgrouse

Walvis Bay and the Namib Desert

The cold Benguela Current, which flows north along Namibia's coast, supports one of the world's richest marine environments. It also moderates temperatures on the Namib coastline, and thus frost does not occur. Fog from the ocean provides much-needed moisture to endemic animals and plants in this otherwise hyper-arid environment, which receives less than 50mm average annual rainfall! The gravel plains, huge sand dunes, rocky hills and mountains of the Namib inland of Walvis Bay have sparse grass and low shrubs. Trees occur only along seasonal rivers.

The harbour town of Walvis Bay and the more tourist-oriented coastal town of Swakopmund 30km north host several tidal lagoon mudflats, artificial salt pans and estuarine and marine coastal habitats that together form the most extensive coastal wetland in southern Africa, hosting upwards of 100,000 waterbirds in summer, including vast numbers of migrant waders and Lesser and Greater flamingoes. The locally common Damara Tern is easily seen over the lagoon and salt pans at Walvis Bay.

The only true endemic of Namibia, the Dune Lark, is restricted to the central Namib dune sea, and is locally common in dune and inter-dune areas with sparse grass and shrub cover. It can be found among small (hummock) dunes a short drive east of Walvis Bay in the Kuiseb River delta. North of the seasonal Kuiseb River the central dune sea gives way to vast gravel plains that host a range of desert-adapted near-endemics such as Gray's and Benguela Long-billed larks, Tractrac Chat, Ruppell's Korhaan and Namaqua Sandgrouse.

A bit more than an hour's drive inland from Swakopmund one enters the escarpment zone, where the granite inselbergs of Spitzkop and the Erongo Mountains host near-endemics such as Herero Chat, Monteiro's and Damara Red-billed hornbills, Ruppell's Parrot, Bradfield's Swift, Rockrunner, Hartlaub's Spurfowl and White-tailed Shrike.

N DENNIS/IMAGES OF AFRICA

Blue Crane

Kori Bustard

Etosha National Park

Namibia's most famous national park and game reserve is also an excellent birding destination. This massive park (2.3 million hectares) has a reliable road network providing access to a range of different habitats, including grasslands, dwarf shrub and tree savannas, dolomite hills, waterholes and seasonally flooded salt pans. The park attracts large numbers of tourists in the dry winter months, when wildlife tends to concentrate around the permanent waterholes. However, birders will enjoy the wet summer months when the seasonal pans and surrounding plains fill with water and harbour large numbers of migrant birds, and protected species such as Wattled and Blue cranes and several stork species are readily seen. Near-endemics such as Bare-cheeked Babbler, Violet Wood-hoopoe and Ruppell's Parrot are common at the Halali Rest Camp, as are Northern Black Korhaan and several lark species on the plains further west. Kori Bustards and Secretarybirds are also easy to find on the plains, and the Bateleur is one of the more common eagles seen soaring overhead. The Namutoni area in the east is good for Black-faced Babbler, and the pans in the vicinity are excellent for a wide range of ducks and other wetland species.

Bateleur

White-faced Duck

GLOSSARY

Aigrette A plume of feathers on the rump of a breeding egret.

Alien A bird that is not indigenous to the area.

Breeding endemic A species that breeds only in a particular region but undertakes movements or migrations during the non-breeding season such that a measurable proportion of the population leaves the region.

Cap Area encompassing the forehead and crown.

Casque A helmet or helmet-like process on the bill.

Cere Coloured bare skin at the base of the upper mandible.

Colonial Associating in close proximity, while roosting, feeding or nesting.

Decurved Curving downwards.

Display A pattern of behavior in which the bird attracts attention while it is defending its territory or courting a female, for example.

Eclipse plumage Dull plumage attained during a transitional moult, after the breeding season and before they acquire brighter plumage.

Endemic Restricted to a certain region.

Eye-ring Circle of coloured feathers immediately behind the eye.

Feral Species that have escaped from captivity and now live in the wild.

Flush To rouse and put to flight.

Form Colour variation within a species.

Gorget A band of distinctive colour on the throat.

Immature A bird that has moulted its juvenile plumage but has not yet attained full adult plumage.

Juvenile The first full-feathered plumage of a young bird.

Migrant A species that undertakes long-distance flights between its wintering and breeding areas.

Moustachial stripes Lines running from the base of the bill to the sides of the throat.

Near-endemic A species whose range is largely restricted to a region but extends slightly outside its borders.

Parasitise When a bird lays its eggs in the nest of another species for the purposes of incubation.

Plumage Feathering of a kind.

Primaries The outermost major flight feathers of the wing.

Range A bird's distribution.

Resident A bird that occurs throughout the year in a region and is not known to undertake migration.

Rufous Reddish-brown.

Secondaries Flight feathers of the wing, adjoining the primary feathers.

Shield Bare patch of skin at the base of the bill and on the forehead. Often brightly coloured.

Speculum A patch of bright plumage on the secondaries of ducks.

Summer visitor A bird that is absent from the region during the winter.

Supercilium A stripe above the eye of a bird.

Territory An area that a bird establishes and subsequently defends from others.

Vagrant Rare and accidental to the region.

Vent The area from the belly to the undertail coverts.

PARTS OF A BIRD

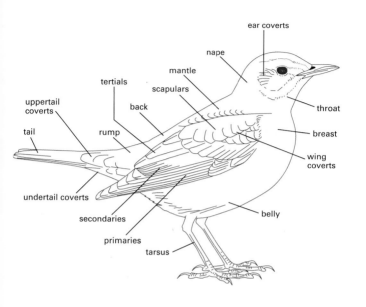

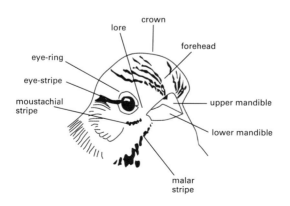

imm.

Southern Giant Petrel
Macronectes giganteus

L 86–100cm Has an all-white phase, unlike the otherwise similar Northern Giant Petrel. When dark brown phase is seen close inshore near seal colonies, *its powerful lumbering flight and hump-backed appearance* aid identification. At close range dark green (not brown) bill tip distinguishes it. Imm. is dark, becoming lighter with age. Emits harsh grunts when squabbling over food. Year-round visitor; more common in winter. **REUSENELLIE (A) RIESENSTURMVOGEL (G)**

P RYAN (BOTH)

White-chinned Petrel
Procellaria aequinoctialis

L 51–58cm Considerably larger than all other dark brown petrels. Diagnostic *white chin and long, robust pale greenish bill with black saddle* are visible at close range. Has a towering, careening flight action high above the waves, regularly venturing close inshore around the coast where it can be seen, quite frequently, following fishing trawlers. Normally silent, but utters a fast 'tititit' when alarmed. Common year-round visitor, but more regularly seen during winter. **BASSIAAN (A) WEISSKINN-STURMVOGEL (G)**

Sooty Shearwater   *Puffinus griseus*

L 40–46cm Diagnostic *silvery linings to underwings* differentiate it from all other dark shearwaters. Sexes alike. Flight is swift and direct, with rapid wingbeats interspersed with short glides when it banks over the waves and flashes its silvery underwings. Seen in coastal waters throughout the year, foraging on small shoaling fish. Silent at sea. The most common shearwater over these coastal waters. **MALBAARTJIE (A) DUNKLER STURMTAUCHER (G)**

Wilson's Storm-Petrel
Oceanites oceanicus

L 15–19cm Very *small dark petrel with a large, square white rump.* Long legs project beyond tail in flight and are obvious, dangling below bird when feeding, but can be retracted into belly plumage. Yellow webbing on feet is hard to see. Flight swallow-like and direct, with frequent glides, but varies with wind strength. Sometimes occurs close inshore but mostly deep ocean. Not uncommon during winter. **GEWONE STORMSWAEL (A) BUNTFUSS-STURMSCHWALBE (G)**

Cape Gannet
Morus capensis

L 84–95cm In ad. all-white plumage contrasts with black flight feathers and black pointed tail. Has *long, dagger-shaped pale grey bill.* Nape and sides of the neck straw yellow. Imm. is dark brown version of ad., progressing through mottled brown and white stages. Utters a 'warrra-warrra-warrra' call when feeding in flocks at sea as well as at br. colonies. Regularly seen along the coast, but does not range very far out to sea. Breeds on islands off the Namibian coast. **WITMALGAS (A) KAPTÖLPEL (G)**

imm.

PETER FODOR/SHUTTERSTOCK.COM

Great White Pelican
Pelecanus onocrotalus

L 140–178cm A large white bird with contrasting *black primary and secondary feathers and a bright yellow pouch.* Assumes a pinkish flush in br. season. Imm. dark brown; young birds lighten with age. Guttural sounds can be heard from br. colonies; otherwise silent. Frequently seen flying in 'V' formation and habitually fishes in groups. Occurs in coastal estuaries and close inshore between Sandwich Harbour and Swakopmund. Seen less often on fresh water. **WITPELIKAAN (A) ROSAPELIKAN (G)**

imm.

Greater Flamingo
Phoenicopterus ruber

L 125–165cm Predominantly white, with a small body in relation to its long legs and long neck. In flight shows brilliant red patches on forewings. In comparison with Lesser Flamingo is larger, less red, and has diagnostic *large pink bill with a black tip*. Imm. is sandy brown, lacking red in the wings and has grey-and-black bill. Call is a goose-like honking. Common in coastal areas and in Etosha, frequenting shallow freshwater lakes, salt pans and estuaries.
GROOTFLAMINK (A) FLAMINGO (G)

Lesser Flamingo
Phoenicopterus minor

L 90–125cm Much smaller and redder than Greater Flamingo. *Dark red, black-tipped bill appears all black when seen at a distance*, further differentiating the two. Imm. is smaller than imm. Greater Flamingo, with a darker, stubbier bill and greyish-brown body. Found in flocks with the Greater Flamingo at freshwater lakes, salt pans and estuaries. Common in coastal regions and breeds at Etosha.
KLEINFLAMINK (A) ZWERGFLAMINGO (G)

White-breasted Cormorant
Phalacrocorax lucidus

L 85–95cm By far the largest cormorant in the region. Ad. has glossy black plumage, *white breast and throat and bright yellow patch at base of the bill*. Shows white flank patches in br. season. Imm. dark brown with variable amounts of white on the underparts. Normally silent, but utters grunts and squeals during br. season. A common coastal bird; avoids feeding over the ocean, preferring sheltered bays and inland freshwater areas. **WITBORSDUIKER (A) WEISSBRUSTKORMORAN (G)**

imm

P RYAN (MAIN IMAGE)

Bank Cormorant
Phalacrocorax neglectus

L 74–76cm Larger and more robust than Cape Cormorant, from which it differs in having *dull black plumage and a thick woolly-textured neck*, and by lacking the pale patch at base of the bill. Has *tuft of erectile feathers on forehead resembling a small rounded crest*. Shows white flecks on head and diagnostic white rump during br. Imm. lacks white flecks on head and has a duller eye. Call is a wheezy 'wheeee', given when alighting near its nest. Near-endemic. Found on coastal waters and offshore islands. **BANKDUIKER (A) KÜSTENSCHARBE (G)**

Cape Cormorant
Phalacrocorax capensis

L 60–65cm Intermediate in size between Bank and Crowned cormorants. Ad. has *glossy blue-black plumage with bright yellow-orange patch at base of bill*. Patch brightens during br. season. Imm. is dowdy brown, with slightly paler underparts. Utters various 'gaaaa' and 'geeee' noises during br. season. The most abundant marine cormorant in the region. Near-endemic. Found in large concentrations on br. platforms along the coast or flying in straight lines to and from feeding areas. **TREKDUIKER (A) KAPKORMORAN (G)**

imm.　　　ad.

Crowned Cormorant
Phalacrocorax coronatus

L 50–55cm Endemic to Benguela upwelling region. Marine counterpart of the Reed Cormorant, with slightly shorter tail. Ad. has *orange-red face, longer forehead crest (in br. plumage) and less contrasting back scaling*. Juv. has brown-washed (not white, as in Reed Cormorant) underparts, especially on throat and breast. Calls are cackles and hisses at colonies; otherwise silent. Found on offshore islands, coast, estuaries and lagoons. Locally common. **KUIFKOPDUIKER (A) WAHLBERGSCHARBE (G)**

imm.

P. RYAN (INSET)

imm.

Reed Cormorant
Phalacrocorax africanus

L 50–56cm Small black cormorant with pale spotting on the back. *Tail is long, unmarked and proportionately longer* than that of White-breasted Cormorant. In br. plumage, ad. shows yellow-orange face patch and throat and displays small erectile crest on the forehead. Imm. is brownish-grey above, with white underparts. Roosts and breeds colonially. Silent, except for cackles and hisses at br. colonies. Frequents freshwater dams, lakes and rivers. Rarely seen at the coast. **RIETDUIKER (A) RIEDSCHARBE (G)**

African Darter
Anhinga rufa

L 80–92cm Resembles a cormorant but has long *egret-like neck with a slender head and elongated pointed bill.* Ad. male in br. plumage shows rufous head and neck, with a long white stripe running from eye onto the neck. Female and non-br. male are pale brown on face and throat. Imm. has white head that darkens with age.Call is a distinctive croaking.Uncommon to common in permanent wetlands throughout Namibia. **SLANGHALSVOËL (A) SCHLANGENHALSVOGEL (G)**

imm.

African Spoonbill
Platalea alba

L 86–92cm *Long, flattened, spoon-shaped red-and-grey bill* is diagnostic. *Legs, feet and face bright red.* In flight, differs from egrets and herons in flying with neck outstretched, not tucked into the shoulders. Wades in shallow water, sweeping its partly opened, specialised bill from side to side to feed. Imm. is duller with dark-tipped flight feathers and a pinkish bill. When alarmed utters a low 'kaark'. Found in permanent wetlands throughout Namibia. **LEPELAAR (A) AFRIKANISCHER LÖFFLER (G)**

imm.

African Sacred Ibis
Threskiornis aethiopicus

L 66–84cm White, with an *unfeathered black head and neck, and long, decurved black bill*. Black-edged flight feathers give the wings a narrow black border in flight. In br. season naked skin on underwing turns scarlet and flank feathers turn yellow. Imm. has white feathering on the neck. Normally silent but croaks loudly at br. colonies. Occurs in permanent wetlands, but more common in northeastern Namibia. **SKOORSTEENVEËR (A) HEILIGER IBIS (G)**

Hadeda Ibis
Bostrichia hagedash brevirostris

L 76–85cm *B. h. brevirostris*, the race of *B. hagedash* in the Zambezi Region, is considered a full species by some. Has a white eye and is darker with a longer bill than the southern race. Bronzy sheen on shoulders is more pronounced and extends over rump and tail. White malar stripe is more striking. Noisy on flights to and from roost trees, giving its distinctive 'ha-ha, ha-ha, de-da' call. Uncommon, except in permanent wetlands in Kavango and Zambezi regions. Recently vagrant in Windhoek wetlands. Usually in small parties. **HADEDA (A) HAGEDASCH-IBIS (G)**

southern race

Glossy Ibis
Plegadis falcinellus

L 55–65cm A rather *small, slender ibis with long legs. Appears black from a distance*. Br. ad.'s head, neck and body are *dark chestnut; wings, back and tail are dark glossy green with bronze and purple highlights*. Has narrow white line around base of bill. Non-br. ad. has pale-flecked head and neck. Juv. resembles non-br. ad., but body is dull sooty brown. Normally silent; gives low guttural 'kok-kok-kok' when br. More common than Hadeda Ibis in permanent wetlands of Namibia. **GLANSIBIS (A) BRAUNER SICHLER (G)**

imm.

Grey Heron
Ardea cinerea

L 90–100cm Large, long-legged greyish heron, with *white head and neck and a black eye-stripe* that ends on the nape in a wispy black crest. Bill is dagger-shaped and yellow. Imm. lacks eye-stripe and crest and has darker bill and yellow upper legs. In flight ad. distinguished from Black-headed Heron by its uniform grey underwing. Call is a harsh 'kraauunk'. Mostly solitary except in br. period. Common in coastal regions and inland freshwater areas. **BLOUREIER (A) GRAUREIHER (G)**

Black-headed Heron
Ardea melanocephala

L 86–94cm *Unmistakable; black-topped head and hindneck contrast with white throat.* Imm. grey (not black) on head and neck and told from imm. Grey Heron by its dark legs and thighs and, in flight, its *contrasting black-and-white (not uniform grey) underwing*. Gives loud 'aaaaark' call, hoarse cackles and bill clapping at the nest. More often seen stalking through open grasslands than near water. Thinly distributed throughout Namibia but more common in the north. **SWARTKOPREIER (A) SCHWARZKOPFREIHER (G)**

imm.

Great Egret
Ardea alba

L 85–92cm *Large white egret with large heavy bill; gape extends behind eye.* Larger and heavier-billed than Western Cattle Egret. Lacks yellow toes of much smaller Little Egret. Structure recalls larger heron. Legs and feet are black at all times. In br. plumage has elaborate plumes, black bill and lime-green lores. Non-br. birds have yellow bill. Call is a low heron-like 'waaaark'. Found chiefly on lakes, dams, estuaries and lagoons. Locally common. **GROOTWITREIER (A) SILBERREIHER (G)**

Little Egret
Egretta garzetta

L 55–65cm A small white heron distinguished from all other herons in Namibia by its *black legs and contrasting yellow toes. Bill is slender and always black.* In br. plumage shows white head plumes and aigrettes on lower back. Imm. lacks plumes and aigrettes. Feeds by dashing to and fro in shallow water, stabbing at prey. Call is a harsh 'waaark' similar to that of other egrets. Occurs in coastal and freshwater areas; breeds in colonies in reedbeds. **KLEINWITREIER (A) SEIDENREIHER (G)**

Western Cattle Egret
Bubulcus ibis

L 48–54cm Small, compact egret with *short bill, neck and legs.* Legs olive-yellow; bill yellow. Ad. has *shaggy bib of plumes on crown, mantle and breast;* buff areas increase in br. season, but less extensive than Squacco Heron's. Pre-br. birds have reddish bill and legs. Juv. has black legs that soon pale. Gives heron-like 'aaaark' or 'pok-pok'. Roosts in flocks, commuting up to 20km to feeding areas. Breeds in colonies, usually with other egrets, herons, cormorants and ibises. Common resident in north and a nomad in a range of open habitats. **VEEREIER (A) KUHREIHER (G)**

br.

non-br.

Slaty Egret
Egretta vinaceigula

L 48–58cm *Dark grey with rufous throat.* Has a variable amount of greenish-yellow on the toes and legs. Does not use wings to shade water when feeding. Eyes yellow (black in pre-br. birds). Juv. paler; lacks head and breast plumes; legs greenish-grey. Gives heron-like squawks and a 'krrr-krrr-krrr' in alarm. Breeds in colonies of up to 200 pairs. Locally common resident and local nomad at marshes and vegetated lake shores. **ROOIKEELREIER (A) BRAUNKEHLREIHER (G)**

IAN WHITE

Rufous-bellied Heron
Ardeola rufiventris

L 38–40cm Small heron, with a *sooty head and breast and rufous belly, wings and tail*. Skulking; normally seen only when flushed. In flight, bright yellow legs and feet contrast strongly with dark underparts. Bill yellowish-grey with black tip; pre-br. birds have red lores and legs. Female duller, with pale throat. Juv. dull brown, with buff streaking on breast and throat. Call is a heron-like 'waaaaak'. Fairly common resident in the permanent wetlands of northern Namibia.
ROOIPENSREIER (A) ROTBAUCHREIHER (G)

imm.

Squacco Heron
Ardeola ralloides

L 42–46 A small *buff-and-white heron, with heavy dark-tipped bill.* At rest, appears mostly buff-and-brown, with white underparts. In flight, white wings and tail are prominent. Smaller and more compact than Western Cattle Egret, with broader wings. Gives a low-pitched 'kruuk' and rattling 'kek-kek-kek'. More common in the north and follows seasonal floods. Occurs in various wetlands. Breeds in mixed colonies in trees or reedbeds.
RALREIER (A) RALLENREIHER (G)

A. FRONEMAN/AFRIPICS (MAIN IMAGE)

juv.

Black-crowned Night-Heron
Nycticorax nycticorax

L 58–64cm *Black crown, nape and back contrast with grey wings and tail and white underparts.* Juv. grey-brown (not tawny), with white spotting above, and lacks black crown and moustachial stripes. Call is a harsh 'kwok' in flight. Roosts communally in reeds and trees during the day, flying out at dusk to feed. Found on rivers and in permanent wetlands. Fairly common resident in the north. **GEWONE NAGREIER (A) NACHTREIHER (G)**

Abdim's Stork
Ciconia abdimii

L 76–81cm A black-and-white stork, distinguished from similar storks by diagnostic *white lower back and rump*, as well as *greenish legs, with pink ankle* and greenish bill. At close range, red joints and blue face visible. Imm. has dark red bill and is duller than ad. Normally silent but gives weak two-noted whistle at roosts. Common summer visitor; often occurs in large flocks in open fields and on agricultural lands.
KLEINSWARTOOIEVAAR (A) ABDIMSSTORCH (G)

D. DANIELS/WIKIMEDIA/CC BY SA 3.0

Marabou Stork
Leptoptilos crumeniferus

L 130–150cm Huge, with a *naked head and neck, massive bill and bare, fleshy pink pouch*. In flight, enormous black wings contrast with white body, and head is tucked into the shoulders. Imm. very similar to ad. but head and neck covered with sparse woolly down. Gives a low hoarse croak when alarmed and claps its bill when displaying. Inflated pouch warns off other birds. Primarily a scavenger. Usually seen in major game reserves, soaring with vultures or scavenging at lion kills. Wide-ranging over bushveld. **MARABOE (A) MARABU (G)**

Hamerkop
Scopus umbretta

L 50–58cm *Hammer-shaped head is unmistakable.* Dark brown, with long legs, a heavy crest and large black bill. In flight, looks hawk-like with its finely barred tail, but long bill and legs preclude confusion with birds of prey. Builds a huge domed nest in a tree or on a cliff, with a small, round, downward-facing entrance from one end of the structure. Gives a sharp 'kiep' call in flight. Common in freshwater dams and rivers, swampy regions and seasonally flooded areas; more abundant in the north. **HAMERKOP (A) HAMMERKOPF (G)**

juv. / br.

K. BILLINGTON/WIKIMEDIA/CC BY SA 3.0

Great Crested Grebe
Podiceps cristatus

L 45–56cm A large, long-necked grebe. Ad. unmistakable, *with dark double crest and rufous-edged ruff ringing sides of the head.* Ruff of non-br. ad. smaller and paler. Juv. has black-and-white striped head. In flight (rare) has conspicuous white secondaries and lesser coverts. Wings long and thin; flies with neck extended and legs trailing. Gives a barking 'rah-rah-rah' call, growls and grunts. Found at large dams, pans and saltworks; rarely in estuaries and bays. Locally common. **KUIFKOPDOBBERTJIE (A) HAUBENTAUCHER (G)**

br. / non-br.

Black-necked Grebe
Podiceps nigricollis

L 28–33cm Smaller than Great Crested Grebe but larger than Dabchick. Br. ad. has black head and throat and *conspicuous golden ear tufts.* Throat and cheeks of non-br. ad. and imm. are *whitish, not greyish* as in Little Grebe. Normally silent, but gives a soft mellow trill during display. Often seen in huge numbers at the Walvis Bay salt pans. Occurs inland during seasonal flooding of wetlands and frequents reed-fringed ponds. **SWARTNEKDOBBERTJIE (A) SCHWARZHALSTAUCHER (G)**

br. / non-br.

D. KEATS/WIKIMEDIA/CC BY 2.0 (INSET)

Little Grebe (Dabchick)
Tachybaptus ruficollis

L 20cm One of the smallest aquatic birds in Namibia. *Pale creamy spot at base of bill is diagnostic.* Dark, with *chestnut sides to neck* in br. season. Non-br. ad. and imm. greyish-brown, but imm. may show black and white stripes on the cheeks. Call is a noisy, often-heard, whinnying trill. Dives frequently, often emerging with just the head showing above water. Common on most permanent freshwater wetlands. **KLEINDOBBERTJIE (A) ZWERGTAUCHER (G)**

White-faced Whistling Duck
Dendrocygna viduata

L 43–48cm *Long-necked, dark brown duck with diagnostic white face.* Stands erect. Dark chestnut brown on breast, with finely barred flanks. Apart from the white face (which can be stained brown), appears all-dark in flight. Juv. lacks white face. Gives characteristic three-noted wispy 'whit we-weeer' whistle. Found on freshwater dams, pans, rivers and open water in permanent wetlands in northern Namibia. Often in large flocks. **NONNETJIE-EEND (A) WITWENENTE (G)**

African Pygmy Goose
Nettapus auritus

L 30–33cm *Tiny duck with diagnostic orange breast and flanks, white face and dark greenish upperparts.* Male has bright yellow bill and lime green neck patch, neatly bordered in black. Female and juv. duller, with indistinct head markings. In flight, has large white patch formed by inner secondaries and greater coverts. Call is a soft, repeated 'tsui-tsui'. Frequents freshwater dams, pans and rivers of wetlands in northern Namibia. Locally common in Zambezi and Kavango regions. **DWERGGANS (A) AFRIKANISCHE ZWERGGANS (G)**

♂

♀

M. BOOYSEN

Spur-winged Goose
Plectropterus gambensis

L 75–100cm *Large black goose with variable white on face, throat, belly and forewings.* Bill, face and legs pink-red. In flight, large size and white on forewing separate it from Comb Duck. Male up to twice the size of female, with more extensive bare face and wattles. Juv. browner. Gives feeble wheezy whistle in flight. Frequents wetlands and adjacent grasslands and grazes on grass and other vegetable matter, often at night. Common, mostly in the north. **WILDEMAKOU (A) SPORENGANS (G)**

Comb (Knob-billed) Duck
Sarkidiornis melanotos

L 56–76cm Unmistakable large duck with *grey speckled head and contrasting blue-black and white plumage.* In flight, wings are black with no markings, although female shows a little white on lower back. Male is larger than female, and in br. season has conspicuous comb on bill. Imm. has dark speckling on the white areas. Can give a whistle but is usually silent. May be seen on any still freshwater body, and on larger rivers in north. **KNOBBELEEND (A) HÖCKERENTE (G)**

Egyptian Goose
Alopochen aegyptiacus

L 60–75cm *Dark brown mask around the eye, white forewings and brown patch on chest* are diagnostic of this small 'goose'. Neck and legs are longer than those of South African Shelduck. A thin dark line through white forewing is visible in flight. Imm. lacks brown mask around eye and the brown breast patch. Very noisy and aggressive in flocks, giving loud honking and hissing noises. Common in freshwater habitats and coastal areas, but not found in dry parts. **KOLGANS (A) NILGANS (G)**

South African Shelduck
Tadorna cana

L 60–65cm A large *russet-coloured duck, with black bill and legs.* Male has diagnostic grey head; female has variable white-and-grey head. Both sexes show white forewings in flight but no black dividing line as in Egyptian Goose. Imm. resembles ad. Gives various honks and hisses. Frequents freshwater dams, seasonal pans, rivers and coastal areas. Fairly common in southern and central Namibia, except in very arid areas. Uncommon in northern Namibia. **KOPEREEND (A) GRAUKOPF-ROSTGANS (G)**

Yellow-billed Duck   *Anas undulata*

L 51–58cm *Bright yellow bill with black saddle is distinctive.* Looks dark from a distance, but is mottled dark brown. At close range, pale feather edges give scaled appearance. In flight, has grey underwings and blue-green speculum narrowly edged with white. Male gives a rasping hiss; female quacks. Largely absent from arid areas. Uncommon in permanent wetlands of northeastern Namibia and a vagrant to freshwater dams further south. **GEELBEKEEND (A) GELBSCHNABELENTE (G)**

Cape Shoveler   *Anas smithii*

L 48–54cm An elongate duck distinguished by its *black spatulate bill*, which appears longer than the head. Finely speckled grey-brown plumage. *Legs rich yellow-orange.* In flight, *powder blue forewings* are very conspicuous. Male has paler head and yellower eyes than female; overall, female is darker than male. Imm. resembles female. Gives quacks and rasping calls. Found in small groups on fresh water, preferably with surface vegetation. Uncommon throughout Namibia and absent from arid areas. **KAAPSE SLOPEEND (A) KAPLÖFFELENTE (G)**

Southern Pochard
Netta erythrophthalma

L 48–51cm Fairly large. *Male dark brown, with chestnut-brown flanks, pale blue bill and red eyes.* Female dark brown, with pale patch at base of bill and pale crescent behind eye. Juv. resembles female, but lacks crescent. Both sexes have paler vents and, in flight, a distinct white wing bar extending onto primaries. Differs in shape from Maccoa Duck and bill is more slender. Male makes a whining sound; female quacks. Locally common at dams and wetlands, including alkaline lakes. **BRUINEEND (A) ROTAUGENENT (G)**

Red-billed Teal   *Anas erythrorhyncha*

L 43–48cm A medium-sized, brown-and-buff mottled duck, with diagnostic *dark cap, pale cheeks and red bill*. Dark cap distinguishes it from the paler Cape Teal. In flight, shows pale secondaries and a buff speculum. Imm. bird is duller than ad. Female's call is a soft quack; male gives a soft nasal whistle. Sexes similar. Very common and occurs in mixed flocks on large stretches of open fresh water. **ROOIBEKEEND (A) ROTSCHNABELENTE (G)**

Cape Teal   *Anas capensis*

L 44–48cm The palest duck in the region. Easily identified by its *mottled greyish plumage and slightly upturned pink bill*. In flight, wing pattern shows two broad white stripes bordering a small green speculum. Imm. is pale grey. Call is a thin high-pitched whistle, usually given in flight. Mostly occurs in mixed flocks. Found throughout the region, especially in drier areas, on any open stretch of fresh or saline water. **TEELEEND (A) KAPENTE (G)**

Hottentot Teal   *Anas hottentota*

L 30–35cm Diminutive; resembles Red-billed Teal, but has *blue (not red) bill and a dark smudge on its creamy cheeks*. In flight, male has a green speculum with white secondaries, and a black-and-white underwing. Female lacks the green speculum. Juv. duller than ad. Call consists of high-pitched quacks on taking flight, but generally silent. Found mainly inland on small water bodies, often close to floating vegetation. Locally common resident but rare in the southwest of its range. **GEVLEKTE EEND (A) HOTTENTOTTENENTE (G)**

Maccoa Duck
Oxyura maccoa

L 48–51cm The only stiff-tailed duck in the region. Br. male has *chestnut body, black head and heavy blue bill*. Female and eclipse male are dark brown, with pale stripe under the eye and paler throat, giving the head a striped appearance (female Southern Pochard has pale crescent behind eye). In flight, upperwing is uniform dark brown. Sits low in the water, with stiff tail often cocked at a 45° angle. Gives a peculiar nasal trill. Found on freshwater dams and lagoons. Locally common, but sparsely distributed.
BLOUBEKEEND (A) MACCOA-ENTE (G)

White-backed Vulture
Gyps africanus

L 90–100cm Seen from above, *white lower back* contrasts with the dark upperwing. Imm. much darker than ad. and shows less contrast between flight feathers and wing linings. Call is a harsh cackling; emits hissing noises when feeding at the nest. Most frequently seen in flight, riding thermals or searching the ground for kills. Occurs in open savanna parkland and most commonly over bushveld and in larger game reserves. Critically endangered; rare in northern woodlands.
WITRUGAASVOËL (A) WEISSRÜCKENGEIER (G)

Lappet-faced Vulture
Torgos tracheliotus

L 98–115cm The most common vulture in the Namib. Has a diagnostic *bare red-skinned face and throat*. Identified in flight by its white thighs and white bar running along the forepart of underwing. Imm. dark brown all over. High-pitched whistles heard during display. Nests on treetops, solitarily or in small scattered colonies. Found in thornveld and shows a preference for drier regions, but rare outside major game reserves.
SWARTAASVOËL (A) OHRENGEIER (G)

A. FRONEMAN/IMAGES OF AFRICA, M. BOOYSEN (INSET)

White-headed Vulture
Trigonoceps occipitalis

L 92–96cm A strikingly coloured vulture; ad. has diagnostic *white belly, extending as a white line along trailing edge of underwing coverts.* Ad. female also has white inner secondaries and tertials. Head angular, white, with naked pink face; bill orange-red, with pale blue cere. Juv. dark brown, with a narrow whitish line along trailing edge of underwing coverts. Gives high-pitched chattering. Found in open savanna in widely spaced pairs. **WITKOPAASVOËL (A) WOLLKOPFGEIER (G)**

imm.

African Fish Eagle   *Haliaeetus vocifer*

L 63–73cm Large broad-winged eagle with a short tail. Ad. unmistakable: *black-and-chestnut plumage, with white head, breast and tail.* Juv. dark brown, with white patches on head, belly, underwing coverts and primary bases; tail white, with brown tip. With age, head and breast gradually whiten. Gives ringing 'kyow-kow-kow', with head thrown back, from perches or in flight; male's call is higher pitched. Common on perennial rivers and freshwater dams in Namibia. **VISAREND (A) SCHREISEEADLER (G)**

imm.

Bateleur   *Terathopius ecaudatus*

L 55–70cm The most easily identified eagle of the region. *In flight, appears to have virtually no tail.* Flies direct, canting from side to side with its long wings held slightly angled; flaps rarely. *Black, white and chestnut plumage, combined with long wings and a short tail* unmistakable. Male has broader black trailing edge to wing. Imm. a brown version of the ad. with slightly longer tail. Gives loud 'kow-wah'. Fairly common over open tree savanna in the north. Uncommon to rare over commercial farmland. **BERGHAAN (A) GAUKLER (G)**

♂

Verreaux's Eagle
Aquila verreauxii

L 75–95cm Unmistakable, with a diagnostic *white 'V' on the mantle and a white back*. Sexes alike, but female is larger and more extensively white on the back. In flight, wing shape is narrower at the base, broadening out at the central secondaries. Imm. has diagnostic rufous crown and nape, contrasting with darker face and throat. Gives 'keee-uup' when br. Uncommon; favours mountainous and rocky regions frequented by its major prey, dassies. Rare over commercial farmland. **WITKRUISAREND (A) FELSENADLER (G)**

imm.

Martial Eagle
Polemaetus bellicosus

L 78–86cm Huge, with a diagnostic *dark head, throat and upper breast, combined with white, lightly spotted breast and belly and very dark underwing*. Imm. has white 'trousers' and uniform underwings. Gives a rapid 'klooee-klooee-klooee' call in display. Uncommon throughout the region. Frequents a wide range of habitats, including savanna, forest edge and deserts, but is absent from extreme desert areas. **BREËKOPAREND (A) KAMPFADLER (G)**

Wahlberg's Eagle
Aquila wahlbergi

L 55–60cm A small slender eagle, with *short pointed crest on hind crown*. In flight, has diagnostic *long, narrow, square-ended tail and slender straight-edged wings* (lacking marked bulge in secondaries). Usually dark brown, but has pale and intermediate colour morphs. Intra-African migrant in woodland and savanna. **BRUINAREND (A) WAHLBERGS ADLER (G)**

pale morph

dark morph

A. FRONEMAN/IMAGES OF AFRICA (MAIN IMAGE)

A. FRONEMAN (INSET)

Tawny Eagle

Aquila rapax

L 65–76cm At close range, has diagnostic *yellow gape, extending to below the middle of the pale eye. Unbarred to faintly barred tail* also diagnostic in this species. Plumage variable in colour, ranging from streaked dark brown to pale buff. Female is usually darker than male. Imm. rufous brown, fading to buff as it develops into sub-ad. Seldom calls, except for a sharp 'kyow' bark. Found in thornveld and semi-desert areas.
ROOFAREND (A) RAUBADLER (G)

Steppe Eagle

Aquila nipalensis

L 67–82cm Large, with a heavy bill and long broad wings. *Yellow gape extends to back of eye (not middle, as in Tawny Eagle).* Usually dark brown. Ad. has barred tail and brown (not yellow) eye. More common juv. is lighter, with pale bars along the edges of upper- and underwing coverts, pale trailing edge to wing and a pale U-shaped rump patch. Silent in Africa. Uncommon summer Palearctic migrant, mostly in northern Namibia. **STEPPE-AREND (A) STEPPENADLER (G)**

African Hawk Eagle

Aquila spilogaster

L 60–68cm In flight has *mainly white underwing, with black trailing edge.* From above has *dark brown upperwing, with white panels at base of primaries.* Imm. russet below, lightly streaked with black; also shows mainly white underwing. In courtship, gives musical 'klee-klee-klee' call. Pairs hunt and perch together. Frequents open thornveld, woodland and savanna in hilly country. Common but thinly distributed; mostly absent from the south. **GROOTJAGAREND (A) HABICHTSADLER (G)**

Booted Eagle
Aquila pennatus

L 45–55cm *Small, with long square-tipped tail.* Wings and tail broader than in Wahlberg's Eagle. *Has white 'landing lights' where leading edge of wing meets the body.* In the more common pale morph, whitish underwing coverts contrast with dark flight feathers; face mostly brown; throat white. Dark morph is dark brown, except for 'landing lights', pale inner primaries and buffy bar across upperwing coverts. Rufous morph also occurs. Gives a high-pitched 'kee-keeee'. Avoids forests; breeds on cliffs. Uncommon Palearctic migrant, Oct–Apr. **DWERGAREND (A) ZWERGADLER (G)**

dark morph

Brown Snake Eagle
Circaetus cinereus

L 68–75cm Differs from other brown eagles by its *large head, prominent yellow eyes and bare pale legs.* In flight, dark brown underwing coverts contrast with pale flight feathers. Tail is barred. Juv. sometimes paler, with a slightly scaled appearance. Generally silent, but call is a croaking 'hok-hok-hok-hok', given in flight. Found in savanna and woodland. Locally common and nomadic. **BRUINSLANGAREND (A) BRAUNER SCHLANGENADLER (G)**

Black-chested Snake Eagle
Circaetus pectoralis

L 63–68cm Medium-sized; identified in flight by *white body and underwings, black-barred primaries and secondaries, dark brown head and upper breast.* At rest, appears large-headed, with huge bright yellow eyes. Imm. is rich rufous, with barred flight feathers and uniform dark brown tail. Lacks Martial Eagle's black spots on lower breast and belly. High-pitched 'kwo-kwo-kwo-kweeu' call is seldom heard. Widespread. **SWARTBORSSLANGAREND (A) SCHWARZBRUST-SCHLANGENADLER (G)**

M. BOOYSEN/TH. KRAFT/WIKIMEDIA/CC BY SA 2.5 (INSET)

Black Kite
Milvus migrans

L 51–60cm *Long-winged, with long shallowly forked tail.* Distinctive loose flight action, regularly twisting its long tail. Wings are held level, not canted up as in harriers, and are narrower than those of buzzards, with bent wrists. *Bill black, with yellow cere.* Ad. has grey ear coverts (not brown as in Yellow-billed Kite). Juv. has brown face, pale eye, slightly less forked tail and buffy feather margins. Gives shrill whinnying call. Ranges widely. Often in flocks at termite emergences. Common non-br. Palearctic migrant in summer months. **SWARTWOU (A) SCHWARZMILAN (G)**

Yellow-billed Kite
Milvus aegyptius

L 56cm *Has a bright yellow bill and deeply forked tail.* Distinguished from other birds of prey by its forked tail, which it twists in flight, from the horizontal to the near vertical, as it manoeuvres through the air. Imm. has buffy feather margins. Call is a whinnying 'kleeeuw' trill. Ranges from forest edge to grassland; often seen patrolling roads, and frequents towns and cities. Intra-African summer migrant more common in northern Namibia. **GEELBEKWOU (A) SCHMAROTZERMILAN (G)**

TOBI 87/WIKIMEDIA/CC BY SA 3.0, 2.5, 2.0, 1.0 (INSET)

Augur Buzzard
Buteo augur

L 55–60cm Unlike other buzzards has a *white throat, breast, belly and wing linings.* Bill is black; cere, legs and feet are yellow. Female has black on lower throat. Imm. brown above and buffy below, with darker brown streaking. Call is a harsh 'kow-kow-kow', given during display. Commonly found in mountain ranges and hilly country in woodland, savanna and desert; range extends to sea level in arid coastal Namibia. **WITBORSJAKKALSVOËL (A) AUGURBUSSARD (G)**

Steppe Buzzard

Buteo vulpinus

L 46–52cm Easily confused with many similar raptors in the region but most birds show *pale broad crescent across breast.*
Plumage coloration varies from pale brown to almost black. Imm. similar to ad., but has yellow (not brown) eyes and narrower terminal tail bar. Call is a gull-like 'pee-ooo'. Common summer visitor, found in open country and seen perched on telephone poles along roads. Avoids deserts and well-wooded regions.
BRUINJAKKALSVOËL (A) MÄUSEBUSSARD (G)

African Marsh-Harrier

Circus ranivorus

L 45–50cm *Flight feathers and tail barred at all ages* (not always visible from a distance, especially in juvs). Lacks marked sexual dimorphism, but individual variation is great. Larger and broader-winged than similar harriers, with dark (not white) rump. Juv. has pale head and leading edge to upperwing and prominent pale breast bar. Mainly silent; display call is a high-pitched 'fee-ooo'. Frequents marshes, reedbeds and adjacent grassland. Locally common to scarce in the north. **AFRIKAANSE VLEIVALK (A) AFRIKANISCHE ROHRWEIHE (G)**

Black-shouldered Kite

Elanus caeruleus

L 30–33cm Conspicuous, small grey-and-white raptor, with diagnostic *black shoulder patch and deep cherry-red eye.* Commonly seen hovering or sitting on telephone poles flicking its white tail up and down. Imm. more buffy than ad., with brown-and-buff-barred back. Emits high-pitched whistles and harsher 'kek-kek-kek' sounds. Common in all but extreme desert areas, from mountainous regions to open thornveld; also often seen in agricultural lands. **BLOUVALK (A) GLEITAAR (G)**

M BOOYSEN

Lizard Buzzard
Kaupifalco monogrammicus

L 35–37cm Compact; between buzzards and accipiters in size and shape. *White throat with black central stripe diagnostic at all ages.* Ad. has red cere and legs and dark red eye. In flight, shows white rump and one (rarely two) broad white tail bar(s). Bulkier than Gabar Goshawk. Juv. has paler cere and legs and pale fringes to upperpart feathers. Noisy in br. season; gives a 'peoo-peoo' and a 'klioo-klu-klu-klu-klu'. Frequents well-wooded savanna and forest clearings. Locally common resident; nomadic in drier areas. **AKKEDISVALK (A) SPERBERBUSSARD (G)**

Pale Chanting Goshawk
Melierax canorus

L 48–62cm Much larger than the Gabar Goshawk, with proportionately longer legs. In flight, *upperparts show a white rump and white secondaries.* Ad. is light grey above, but paler on the wing coverts. Imm. is dark brown above, streaked and blotched with brown below. Gives a chanting 'kleeuu-kleeuu-klu-klu-klu' call during br. season. The hawk most commonly seen along roadsides in Namibia, from drier areas to the bushveld. **BLEEKSINGVALK (A) WEISSBÜRZEL-SINGHABICHT (G)**

imm.

Dark Chanting Goshawk
Melierax metabates

L 43–50cm *Darker grey than Pale Chanting Goshawk, with grey rump; dark grey lesser upperwing coverts contrast with paler median and greater coverts; secondaries grey.* Other goshawks are smaller, mostly with yellow legs; Gabar Goshawk is smaller, with white rump. Juv. has darker, barred rump than does juv. Pale Chanting Goshawk. Gives piping 'kleeu-kleeu-klu-klu-klu'. Fairly common resident in teak woodlands of northeastern Namibia. **DONKERSINGVALK (A) GRAUBÜRZEL-SINGHABICHT (G)**

Gabar Goshawk *Micronisus gabar*

L 28–36cm Identified in its common grey form by the *white rump, grey throat and breast and red eyes, cere and legs.* Uncommon black form is identified by its red cere and legs. Imm. has rufous-streaked and mottled head and breast, but also shows white rump. Usually silent, but gives high-pitched 'kik-kik-kik-kik-kik' call in display. Perches in the canopy, flying quickly from one tree to the next; seldom soars. Frequents savanna, especially thornveld and semi-arid habitats; the most frequently seen small accipiter in the region. **KLEINSINGVALK (A) GABARHABICHT (G)**

UP KEE/WIKIMEDIA/CC BY SA 2.0

Ovambo Sparrowhawk

Accipiter ovampensis

L 32–40cm Medium-sized, with *yellow-orange legs, orange (or red) cere and red eye.* Grey above, dark tail bars; rump grey. Larger than Shikra, with darker red eye, grey-barred underparts, and along with rare melanistic form has white vertical flecks in tail. Larger than melanistic Gabar Goshawk, with paler legs and cere and richer orange bare parts. Juv. brown above, with white or rufous underparts; pale eyebrow. Br. call is soft 'keeep-keeep-keeep'. Uncommon; savanna and woodland. **OVAMBOSPERWER (A) OVAMBOSPERBER (G)**

Shikra *Accipiter badius*

L 28–30cm Shikra (previously Little Banded Goshawk) differs from Little Sparrowhawk in lacking white rump and tail spots. Distinguished by its *rufous barring below, cherry-red eye and yellow legs.* Imm. brown, with a streaked breast and barred belly. Avoids dense evergreen forests and extremely dry regions. Male's call is a high-pitched 'keewik-keewik-keewik'; female's call is a softer 'kee-uuu'. Common in shrub-and-tree savanna in central and northern Namibia. **GEBANDE SPERWER (A) SCHIKRA (G)**

M. BOOYSEN (MAIN IMAGE)

imm.

imm.

Little Sparrowhawk
Accipiter minullus

L 23–27cm Tiny hawk with a *white rump and 2 white spots on its dark uppertail*. In flight, broad rounded wings and long tail are visible. Imm. brown above, with pear-shaped spots on breast. During br. season male utters high-pitched 'keewik-keewik-keewik' call; female gives a softer 'kew-kew-kew'. Favours open woodland and has adapted to suburbia. Absent from drier regions but is more common in the north.
KLEINSPERWER (A) ZWERGSPERBER (G)

African Harrier-Hawk
Polyboroides typus

L 60–66cm Large, broad-winged, with small head, long legs and loose, floppy flight. Grey above, finely barred below, with bare yellow face extending around eye. In flight, broad black tips to flight feathers and central white tail band are distinctive. Juv. and imm. brown and streaked; unlike brown eagles, show 4–5 (not 6–7) primary 'fingers' in flight. Juv. has bare, greyish face. Woodland, forests and open scrub. Fairly common. In br. season gives whistled 'suuu-eeee-ooo'.
KAALWANGVALK (A) SCHLANGENSPERBER (G)

Peregrine Falcon   *Falco peregrinus*

L 34–44cm Large, *chunky, with pointed wings and relatively short tail*. Has obvious black moustachial stripe and dark, slate-grey upperparts. Heavily streaked with black on lower underparts. Summer migrant race *F. p. pallidus* much larger and paler. Imm. dark brown above and heavily streaked with brown on underparts. Call a loud 'kerchuk-kerchuk'. Frequents wide range of habitats, often hunting over wetlands. **SWERFVALK (A)**
WANDERFALKE (G)

Lanner Falcon
Falco biarmicus

L 36–48cm Medium-sized falcon with a *rufous forehead and crown, thin moustachial stripe and unmarked, pinkish breast.* In flight shows relatively broad wings, rounded at the base and narrowing into points. The tail is longer than that of smaller falcons, giving it a floppier flight action. Imm. has buffy streaked crown and heavily streaked underparts. Gives harsh 'kak-kak-kak-kak-kak' call. Common in most areas, especially in the vicinity of waterholes in game reserves. **EDELVALK (A) LANNERFALKE (G)**

imm.

N. DENNIS/IMAGES OF AFRICA (MAIN IMAGE)

Eurasian Hobby
Falco subbuteo

L 28–36cm In flight long, pointed wings and relatively short tail give it a swift-like appearance. The *black head and moustachial stripe contrast boldly with the white throat.* Has heavily streaked breast, with conspicuous rufous leggings and vent. Imm. lacks rufous leggings and vent. Silent in this region. Found in open, broadleaved woodland savanna. Mostly uncommon summer visitor, chiefly in the north. **EUROPESE BOOMVALK (A) BAUMFALKE (G)**

BIOPALKER/WIKIMEDIA// CC BY SA 3.0-DE

Red-necked Falcon
Falco chicquera

L 30–36cm Small but unmistakable, with *chestnut crown and nape, dark brown moustachial stripes on white cheeks,* and blue-grey upperparts with fine black barring. Tail grey, tipped with a broad, black band. Underparts white, finely barred with black. Breast has rufous wash. Imm. has dark brown head, two buff patches on the nape and pale rufous underparts finely barred with brown. Br. call is a shrill 'ki-ki-ki-ki'. Occurs in palm savanna and arid thornveld. Common but thinly distributed in Namibia. **ROOINEKVALK (A) ROTHALSFALKE (G)**

A. FRONEMAN/IMAGES OF AFRICA

Lesser Kestrel
Falco naumanni

L 26–32cm *Slender. Tail slightly wedge-shaped.* Male has plain chestnut back, grey greater coverts, and buff underparts. Female rufous above, densely barred; paler than Rock Kestrel with grey (not rufous) rump; smaller than Greater Kestrel with more contrast between upper- and underparts. Underparts cream with dark spots; face pale, with dark malar stripes. Juv. more rufous, with less defined malar stripe, rufous (not grey) rump. Open country. Locally abundant Palearctic migrant, Oct– May. High-pitched 'kiri-ri-ri-ri' at communal roosts. **KLEINROOIVALK (A) RÖTELFALKE (G)**

Rock Kestrel
Falco rupicolus

L 30–34cm Male has *black- spotted chestnut back and wings, with spotted and barred underwing.* Female has narrow bands on the tail, which male lacks. Both sexes have *grey head.* Imm. lacks blue-grey on the head and tail. Gives a high-pitched 'kik-kik-kik-kik' call. Occurs in a diverse range of habitats but usually seen in mountainous, rocky terrain. Common but thinly distributed throughout Namibia. **KRANSVALK (A) TURMFALKE (G)**

Greater Kestrel
Falco rupicoloides

L 34–38cm At close range diagnostic *whitish eye* is obvious. Larger and paler brown than Rock Kestrel, with whitish underwing, grey-and-black-barred tail and paler head lacking moustachial stripes. Imm. has brown-barred, rufous tail and dark eye. Usually silent, but gives repeated shrill 'kee-ker-rik' in display. Perches on telephone poles, fences, dead trees or low rocks, hunting from its perch. Found throughout the drier regions, including the desert, as well as in more open bushveld. **GROOTROOIVALK (A) STEPPENFALKE (G)**

M. BODYSEN

Red-footed Falcon   *Falco vespertinus*

L 28–31cm *Small, kestrel-like falcon. Male dark slate grey, with chestnut vent.* Female has rufous head, with small dark facial mask, lightly streaked, buffy underparts and rufous underwing coverts. From above, may resemble Red-necked Falcon, but has narrower, dark tail bar and shape and flight action differ. Juv. has off-white underparts, more streaked than female's. Head whitish, with dark mask and indistinct cap. Grassland and arid savanna. Fairly common Palearctic migrant, mostly Nov–May. Shrill chattering at communal roosts. **WESTELIKE ROOIPOOTVALK (A) ROTFUSSFALKE (G)**

Pygmy Falcon   *Polihierax semitorquatus*

L 18–20cm Distinguished by *its very small size.* Shrike-like in appearance and manner; sits very upright on an exposed perch and hawks insects and lizards. Male has grey upperparts and white underparts. Female has deep chestnut back. White rump is conspicuous in flight. Imm. similar to female but has dull brown back. Call is a noisy 'chip-chip' and 'kik-kik-kik-kik'. Occurs in dry thornveld and semi-desert regions. **DWERGVALK (A) ZWERGFALKE (G)**

P. PICKFORD/IMAGES OF AFRICA

Secretarybird   *Sagittarius serpentarius*

L 1.25–1.50m Might be mistaken for a stork or crane when seen at long range, but *short, hooked bill, black, partly feathered legs and wispy black nape plumes* should rule out confusion. In flight, central tail feathers project well beyond tail and legs. Imm. has shorter tail and yellow, not red, facial skin. Utters a deep croak during aerial display. Pairs often seen hunting over savanna and open grasslands. Fairly common on the grassy plains of the north. **SEKRETARISVOËL (A) SEKRETÄR (G)**

A. FRONEMAN/IMAGES OF AFRICA

Helmeted Guineafowl
Numida meleagris

L 55–60cm A familiar game bird, easily distinguished by its *rotund grey body flecked with white, the naked blue-and-red head* and the bare crown casque. Male's casque is longer than that of female. Imm. has less developed casque and browner body coloration, with enlarged white flecking on the neck. Emits a loud 'krrdi-krrdi-krrdi-krrdi' call and a 'kek-kek-kek-kek' alarm note. Is common throughout the region but absent from extreme desert areas. **GEWONE TARENTAAL (A) HELMPERLHUHN (G)**

A. FRONEMAN/IMAGES OF AFRICA

Orange River Francolin
Francolinus levaillantoides

L 32–35cm In Namibia can only be confused with the smaller Hartlaub's Spurfowl, but differs in having *dark stripes on the head, with deep red spotting and stripes on the breast and underparts.* In flight shows chestnut primaries. Imm. resembles ad. Call is a distinctive, melodious, oft-repeated 'kibitele', usually given at dawn. Frequents grassy and bush-covered hillsides and gullies. Common in the central and northern areas of the region. **KALAHARIPATRYS (A) REBHUHNFRANKOLIN (G)**

Crested Francolin
Dendroperdix sephaena

L 30–35cm Small francolin, with black tail often held cocked at a 45° angle, imparting a bantam-like appearance. *Dark cap contrasts with broad white supercilium*; neck and breast black-spotted; wings and back striped with white. Call is a repeated 'chee-chakla'. Common in north, in woodland and wooded savanna. **BOSPATRYS (A) SCHOPFFRANKOLIN (G)**

Red-billed Spurfowl
Pternistis adspersus

L 35–38cm A dark francolin with diagnostic *yellow eye-ring and dull red bill and legs.* Differs from other dark francolins in being more uniform in colour and slightly paler below, and by lacking any streaking or blotching. Imm. lacks yellow eye-ring. Gives a loud, harsh 'chaa-chaa-chek-chek' call. Found in dry thornveld, open, broadleaved woodland and in thickets along river beds. Less shy than other francolins. Often seen feeding in the open. **ROOIBEKFISANT (A) ROTSCHNABELFRANKOLIN (G)**

Swainson's Spurfowl
Pternistis swainsonii

L 33–38cm A large dark brown spurfowl *with black legs and bare red face and throat.* Breast and flank feathers have thin black central stripes. Dawn crowing is a harsh 'kraae-kraae'. Common in the north in small coveys in savanna and fields. **BOSVELDFISANT (A) SWAINSONFRANKOLIN (G)**

Hartlaub's Spurfowl
Pternistis hartlaubi

L 25–28cm The smallest francolin in the region and near-endemic to Namibia. *Dark cap and contrasting white eyebrow are distinctive in the male.* Has large decurved bill and pale underparts heavily streaked with brown. Female and imm. dull brown, lacking any other distinguishing features. Alarm call is a 'wak-ak-ak-ak'. Frequents rocky outcrops in hilly and mountainous regions. Endemic to Namibia and southern Angola. **KLIPFISANT (A) HARTLAUBFRANKOLIN (G)**

M. BOOYSEN

Coqui Francolin   *Peliperdix coqui*

L 20–26cm *Petite with black bill and yellow legs. Male has plain buffy head with darker crown and heavily barred breast.* Female has neatly defined pale throat and supercilium, and plain buffy breast. Southern nominate-race birds have belly completely barred, but northern races have plain belly. Difficult to flush; shows chestnut wings and outer tail in flight. Gives distinctive, disyllabic 'co-qui'; territorial 'ker-aak, aak, kara-kara-kara', with last notes fading away. Common to locally common in woodlands in northeastern Namibia. **SWEMPIE (A) COQUIFRANKOLIN (G)**

Common Quail   *Coturnix coturnix*

L 16–20cm *Small, rather pale buff game bird, streaked black and white above.* Usually seen when flushed; flight action is very rapid. On the ground, runs swiftly through grass in a hunched position. Underparts are buffy, streaked brown on breast. Male has variable black or russet throat. African *C. c. erlangeri* is a summer-br. intra-African migrant. Call is a repeated, high-pitched 'whit wit-wit'; also gives a shrill 'crwee-crwee' in flight. Found in grassland, fields and croplands. Locally abundant. **AFRIKAANSE KWARTEL (A) WACHTEL (G)**

Red-knobbed Coot   *Fulica cristata*

L 36–44cm *Medium-sized, matt black, duck-like bird with white bill and white unfeathered forehead.* Has two red knobs on the forehead that are more conspicuous in br. season. Imm. similar to imm. Common Moorhen, but is dull brown and lacks white undertail coverts. Call is a harsh, metallic 'claak'. Found on virtually any stretch of fresh water, except in fast-flowing rivers. Common and nomadic in its range, it appears overnight in newly flooded areas. **BLESHOENDER (A) KAMMBLESSHUHN (G)**

Common Moorhen *Gallinula chloropus*

L 30–36cm Dull, sooty black with green legs, red frontal shield and yellow tip to the bill. Imm. is greyish-brown version of the ad. Call is a sharp 'krrik'. Swims freely on virtually any stretch of fresh water surrounded by a thick cover of reeds and grass. Common in freshwater areas, both coastal and inland.
GROOTWATERHOENDER (A) TEICHHUHN (G)

imm.

Lesser Moorhen *Gallinula angulata*

L 22–26cm Smaller and more secretive than Common Moorhen, with *less conspicuous white flank feathers and mainly yellow (not red) bill*. Juv. is sandy-buff (not grey as in juv. Common Moorhen) with dull, yellowish-green bill and legs. Skulking; usually heard rather than seen. Occurs in the permanent wetlands of northern Namibia. Call is a series of hollow notes, 'do do do do do do do'.
KLEINWATERHOENDER (A) ZWERGTEICHHUHN (G)

M. BOOYSEN

African Purple Swamphen
Porphyrio madagascariensis

L 38–46cm A large gallinule, easily identified by *massive red bill, long red legs and purplish coloration*, with turquoise neck and breast and metallic back. Juv. dull brown above and grey below, with large, reddish-brown bill. Found in reedbeds, marshes and flooded grassland. Common in the permanent wetlands of northern Namibia. Gives variety of harsh shrieks, wails and booming notes. **GROOTKONINGRIETHAAN (A) PURPURHUHN (G)**

imm.

Allen's Gallinule   *Porphyrio alleni*

L 26–30cm *Smaller and darker than African Purple Swamphen, with blue (in br. male) or green (in br. female) frontal shield.* Non-br. birds have dull brown shield. Juv. is pale buff-brown, lacks white flank stripes of juv. Common Moorhen and has pale, fleshy legs (not greenish-brown). Found in marshes, rivers and flooded grassland. Locally common resident and summer visitor in the permanent wetlands of northern Namibia. Call comprises six or more rapidly uttered, sharp clicks, 'duk duk duk duk duk duk'. **KLEINKONINGRIETHAAN (A) AFRIKANISCHES SULTANSHUHN (G)**

Black Crake   *Amaurornis flavirostra*

L 18–22cm *A small, furtive, jet-black bird with bright yellow bill and red eyes and legs.* In br. ad. legs and feet are brighter red. Imm. greyish-brown with black bill and dull red legs. Often gives throaty 'chrrooo' and rippling trills. Occurs in marshes and swamps with thick cover of reeds and other aquatic vegetation. More likely to venture from cover into the open at dawn or dusk. Common in permanent wetlands and freshwater bodies throughout Namibia. **SWARTRIETHAAN (A) MOHRENRALLE (G)**

N. DENNIS/IMAGES OF AFRICA

Wattled Crane   *Bugeranus carunculatus*

L 120–170cm Large crane with *white neck and long facial wattles.* Can be identified even at long range by white neck and body contrasting with black belly and grey upperparts. Seldom calls but gives a loud 'kraaank'. Uncommon and local in seasonal pans and permanent wetlands in northern Namibia. Often seen on pans in the Etosha National Park. **LELKRAANVOËL (A) KLUNKERKRANICH (G)**

Common Ostrich
Struthio camelus

H 1.2–2m *The largest bird, both in Namibia and the world. Unlikely to be misidentified. Male is black and white; female and imm. are greyish-brown and white.* If seen alone, young bird might be mistaken for a korhaan but is distinguished by the very thick legs and flattened bill. Male makes nocturnal booming call that sounds like a lion's roar. Domestic and feral in most regions; genuine wild populations probably only occur in the Namib.

VOLSTRUIS (A) STRAUSS (G)

Kori Bustard
Ardeotis kori

L 110–140cm *By far the largest bustard in the region. Its size and lack of any rufous on hindneck and upper mantle, as well as long dark crest, should rule out confusion* with much smaller Ludwig's Bustard, also found in the region. Reluctant to fly unless threatened. Female similar to male but noticeably smaller. Imm. resembles female. When displaying, male emits a deep, resonant 'oom-oom-oom' call. Usually found near cover of trees in dry thornveld, grassland and semi-desert. Common and conspicuous at Etosha.

GOMPOU (A) RIESENTRAPPE (G)

Ludwig's Bustard
Neotis ludwigii

L 80–100cm *Much smaller than Kori Bustard and readily distinguished by its dark cap, dark throat and long, dark grey-brown foreneck.* Lower hindneck is deep russet. Female is noticeably smaller than male. Displaying male inflates its throat, forming a conspicuous balloon of grey feathers. In flight, shows large expanses of white in the wings. Uncommon and nomadic in Namibia, with populations moving from one region to another in response to rains. **LUDWIGPOU (A) LUDWIGSTRAPPE (G)**

A RILEY/ROCKJUMPER BIRDING TOURS

Red-crested Korhaan
Lophotis ruficrista

L 48–50cm Erect, rufous crest is rarely seen unless a displaying male is observed. Both sexes have *black belly, thin neck and chevron* markings on the back. Female bird has mottled brown crown and neck. Imm. resembles female. Male's call is a 'tic-tic-tic', finishing with a loud, whistling 'chew-chew-chew'. Found in dry thornveld, thick bush and grassy areas adjoining thornveld. Common in the bushveld areas of Namibia.
BOSKORHAAN (A) ROTSCHOPFTRAPPE (G)

Northern Black Korhaan
Afrotis afraoides

L 48–52cm Can instantly be recognised by its *black head and body, brown barred upperparts and bright yellow legs.* In flight, shows white patches on the black primaries. Female resembles Red-crested Korhaan, but has thicker neck, yellow (not olive) legs and obvious white wing patches in flight. In display flight, male circles its territory, calling 'karrak, karrak, karrak'. Common to abundant in some areas, especially open grassland and scrub, but absent from true desert.
WITVLERKKORHAAN (A) WEISSFLÜGELTRAPPE (G)

Rüppell's Korhaan   *Eupodotis rueppellii*

L 50–58cm *Pale pinkish-grey with a conspicuous black line running down the centre of foreneck and extending onto breast. Has contrasting black and white facial markings.* Imm. and female not as boldly marked as male, especially on head and throat. Call is a rasping frog-like 'crrok-rrok-rrek', given at dawn and dusk. Near-endemic to the Namib. Usually found in groups of two or three on gravel plains and in semi-scrub desert.
WOESTYNKORHAAN (A) RÜPPELLTRAPPE (G)

Black-winged Stilt
Himantopus himantopus

L 35–40cm A large wader distinguished by the combination of *exceptionally long red legs and long, very thin black bill*. In flight, *black underwings contrast with white underparts and white neck, and the long legs trail conspicuously*. Br. male shows a black nape and crown. Imm. has extensive brown markings on hindneck and head. Call is a short, harsh 'kik-kik'. Common in suitable marshes, vleis, salt pans and flooded areas.
ROOIPOOTELSIE (A) STELZENLÄUFER (G)

Pied Avocet
Recurvirostra avosetta

L 42–45cm A large, black-and-white wader with *long, very thin, upturned bill. Legs are long and pale blue;* feet are partially webbed. In flight, three black patches forming a pied pattern are visible on each upperwing. Imm. has dusky brown (not black) wing patches. Emits a clear 'kooit' call and a 'kik-kik' alarm call. Usually seen in flocks at pans, estuaries, vleis and temporary pools and is common in Namibia, with large flocks found on the coast. **BONTELSIE (A) SÄBELSCHNÄBLER (G)**

African Jacana
Actophilornis africanus

L 25–32cm *Rufous, with a darker belly, white neck and yellow upper breast.* Contrasting black-and-white head pattern highlights the blue frontal shield and bill. Very long toes and toenails allow it to walk over floating vegetation. Imm. duller than ad. and lacks the frontal shield. Call is a noisy, sharp, ringing 'krrrek' with a 'krrrrrk' flight call. Occurs in flooded grasslands and freshwater areas with floating vegetation; common in the moist regions of the north. **GROOTLANGTOON (A)**
BLAUSTIRN-BLATTHÜHNCHEN (G)

African (Black) Oystercatcher
Haematopus moquini

L 42–45cm Endemic to southern Africa. A *large, all-black wader with bright orange bill and eye-ring and dull pink legs*. Ad. may have small white patches on the underparts, visible in flight. No wing markings in ad. Imm. is dowdier than ad. and has less vivid orange bill, tipped with brown. Gives a 'klee-kleeep' call and a fast 'peeka-peeka-peeka' alarm call. Uncommon in Namibia; confined to rocky shores of Namibia's coast and offshore islands. **SWARTTOBIE (A) SCHWARZER AUSTERNFISCHER (G)**

Spotted Thick-knee
Burhinus capensis

L 43cm A nocturnal wader with *large head, big yellow eyes, a short bill with yellow at the base and greenish-yellow legs*. Brown, buff and black spotted upperparts. In flight two small white patches are visible on each upperwing. Imm. resembles ad. The 'whiw-whiw-whiw' call is heard at night; rests in shade by day. Regularly occurs away from water and is common throughout Namibia, except in extreme desert regions. **GEWONE DIKKOP (A) KAPTRIEL (G)**

Water Thick-knee
Burhinus vermiculatus

L 38–41cm Smaller than Spotted Thick-knee, with *plainer, grey-brown plumage*, finely streaked with dark brown, *and a grey wing panel visible on the folded wing at rest and in flight*. Usually found close to water. Juv. more streaked above. Call a rather mournful 'ti-ti-ti-tee-teee-tooo', slowing and dropping in pitch at the end, usually given at night. Common resident and local nomad along river and lake shores. Usually in pairs. **WATERDIKKOP (A) WASSERTRIEL (G)**

Collared Pratincole
Glareola pratincola

L 24–25cm Large, long-winged. *Pale buff throat, (edged black in br. plumage) separates it from other pratincoles.* Underwing coverts dark rufous (not black); secondaries pale-tipped. Graceful flight, showing white rump and deeply forked tail. Juv. lacks defined throat markings and has buff edges to mantle feathers. Gives 'kik-kik' call, especially in flight. Wetland margins and open areas near water in the north. Locally common intra-African and Palearctic migrant. **ROOIVLERKSPRINKAANVOËL (A) BRACHSCHWALBE (G)**

Temminck's Courser
Cursorius temminckii

L 19–21cm *Small, plain rufous courser with broad black patch behind the eye.* Distinguished by *rufous (not grey) hind crown* and black belly patch (not bar) between and in front of the legs. In flight, flight feathers are black above. Underwing is black, with narrow white trailing edge to secondaries. Juv. duller, with lightly speckled underparts and scalloped upperparts. Call is a grating 'keer-keer'. Frequents dry, sparsely grassed and recently burned areas. Locally common nomad and intra-African migrant. **TREKDRAWWERTJIE (A) TEMMINCKRENNVOGEL (G)**

Burchell's Courser   *Cursorius rufus*

L 21–23cm *A plain, buff grey courser with a black and white line extending back from the eye.* Has blue-grey hind crown, rufous crown and nape. White bar on the secondaries and white tip to the outer tail can be seen in flight. Imm. is mottled above with less well-defined lower breast markings than in ad. Call is a harsh, repeated 'wark'. Thinly distributed in dry, sparsely grassed areas. **BLOUKOPDRAWWERTJIE (A) ROSTRENNVOGEL (G)**

Double-banded Courser
Rhinoptilus africanus

L 20–24cm *A small, pale courser with two narrow black breast bands.* Head plain, with creamy eye-stripe. Upperparts scaled; dark back and wing coverts have broad creamy-buff edges. In flight, white rump is visible, and conspicuous chestnut secondaries and inner primaries contrast with dark outer primaries. Juv. has chestnut breast bands. Semi-arid and desert plains. Common resident. Gives thin, rising and falling 'teeu-wee' and a repeated 'kee-kee', mostly at night. **DUBBELBANDDRAWWERTJIE (A) DOPPELBAND-RENNVOGEL (G)**

Blacksmith Plover   *Vanellus armatus*

L 28–31cm *Large, black, white and grey* bird; the easiest plover to identify in southern Africa. Has distinctive, bold wing pattern. Imm. a duller version of the ad., with greyish-brown (not black) feathers. When alarmed, gives a rapid, metallic 'tink-tink' call. Occurs in damp places such as wetland margins and adjoining grasslands, seasonally flooded areas and coastal pools. Common, especially in the wetter north. **BONTKIEWIET (A) WAFFENKIEBITZ (G)**

White-crowned Lapwing
Vanellus albiceps

L 28–32cm A striking, large plover with *long, pendulous, yellow wattles and a blazing white crown extending to nape.* In flight shows mostly white wings, boldly patterned with black. Call a repeated and ringing 'peek-peek'. Uncommon; frequents sandbars along large rivers in the north. Nomadic, moving in response to changing river levels. **WITKOPKIEWIET (A) LANGSPORNKIEBITZ (G)**

Long-toed Lapwing
Vanellus crassirostris

L 29–31cm The only large plover in Namibia to show a *white face, throat and foreneck.* Black extends from nape down side of the neck to form a large black breast band. Striking in flight, where the wings are almost totally white. Call a high-pitched 'tink-tink' Frequents marshes and floodplains in the north and is seasonal in some areas. **WITVLERKKIEWIET (A) LANGZEHENKIEBITZ (G)**

Crowned Plover   *Vanellus coronatus*

L 30cm A large, readily identifiable plover with a *black cap interrupted by a white 'halo .* Black band separates the white belly from sandy brown breast. *Legs and basal part of the bill are bright reddish colour.* Imm. resembles ad., but is less strikingly marked. Gives a loud, grating 'kreeep' call at night. Has no particular affinity for water, preferring drier grasslands, golf courses and playing fields. Fairly common, but absent from the southern part of Namibia. **KROONKIEWIET (A) KRONENKIEBITZ (G)**

African Wattled Lapwing
Vanellus senegallus

L 34–35cm A very large plover with obvious *elongated, bright yellow facial wattles and bright yellow legs.* Greyish-brown overall with a black lower belly bar. In flight, shows a wide white wing bar contrasting with black flight feathers. Call is a repeated, ringing, far-carrying 'keep-keep', often heard at night. Fairly common in the north on various wetland margins and in adjacent fields. **LELKIEWIET (A) SENEGALKIEBITZ (G)**

Grey Plover
Pluvialis squatarola

L 30cm *A dumpy drab grey* wader with *light white speckling on the back and wing coverts.* In flight, from below, shows *black 'armpits'* and, from above, a pale rump and white wing bar. Head relatively large, with a short black bill. In br. plumage has black underparts with black-and-white spangled back. Call is a fluty 'tluuii', lower in pitch in the middle. Favours open or rocky shorelines and coastal wetlands. **GRYSSTRANDKIEWIET (A) KIEBITZREGENPFEIFER (G)**

Caspian Plover
Charadrius asiaticus

L 18–22cm Non-br. birds have *complete (or virtually complete) grey-brown wash across the breast, and broad, buffy supercilium.* Bill is small and thin. In flight, upperparts are uniform, apart from pale bases to inner primaries. In br. plumage has a *black lower border to chestnut breast band, pale eyebrow and throat, and no dark eye patch.* Juv. appears buffy-scaled. Occurs in short grasslands, bare fields and on wetland fringes. Locally common Palearctic migrant, mostly Aug–Apr. **ASIATIESE STRANDKIEWIET (A) WERMUTREGENPFEIFER (G)**

non-br. ♂

br. ♂

M. BOOYSEN (BOTH)

Kittlitz's Plover
Charadrius pecuarius

L 14–16cm A small plover with *black forehead line extending behind the eye to the nape.* Head is less well marked in non-br. plumage, with a pale buffy ring around the crown extending to the nape. Breast creamy buff with a dark shoulder patch. Imm. differs from similar imm. White-fronted Plover by its buffy nape and dark shoulder. Call is a short, clipped 'kittip' trill. Found on both coastal and inland wetlands and in dry, grassy areas. **GEELBORSSTRANDKIEWIET (A) HIRTENREGENPFEIFER (G)**

White-fronted Plover
Charadrius marginatus

L 18cm A *small, very pale plover with a white collar and incomplete breast band.* Paler than Kittlitz's Plover and lacks black forehead markings, but may have a thin black line through the eye and across the forehead. Imm. lacks dark markings on the head and is paler than the ad. Gives a clear 'wiiit' call and a 'tukut' alarm call. Frequents sandy beaches and muddy coastal areas and is common along the Namibian coastal strip. **VAALSTRANDKIEWIET (A) WEISSSTIRN-REGENPFEIFER (G)**

Chestnut-banded Plover
Charadrius pallidus

L 15cm *The smallest, palest plover in the region. Narrow chestnut breast band extends as a thin line onto the crown in male.* Male also has neat black markings on the forehead and lores. These markings are grey in the female. Imm. has duller, usually incomplete breast band and lacks the black-and-chestnut coloration. Call is a single 'tooit'. Frequents salt pans in summer: some birds move to estuaries and coastal wetlands in winter. **ROOIBANDSTRANDKIEWIET (A) FAHLREGENPFEIFER (G)**

Common Ringed Plover
Charadrius hiaticula

L 18–20cm A *small, dark plover with short legs and a white collar above a blackish-brown breast band;* band often incomplete in non-br. plumage. Legs are orange-yellow and bill is usually orange at the base. In flight, white wing bar is obvious. Imm. has duller plumage than ad. and incomplete breast band. Call is a fluty 'tooi'. Found on coastal and inland wetlands, mainly during summer. **RINGNEKSTRANDKIEWIET (A) SANDREGENPFEIFER (G)**

juv.

Three-banded Plover
Charadrius tricollaris

L 18cm The *double black breast band, grey face and conspicuous red eye-ring and base of the bill* are diagnostic. In flight, tail shows white outer tips and edges, and a white terminal bar. Imm. is duller version of ad., lacking the red eye-ring. Call a penetrating, clear 'weet-weet' whistle. Common throughout Namibia in most wetlands, but prefers small water bodies with sandy or pebbly margins. Rare on the open coast. **DRIEBANDSTRANDKIEWIET (A) DREIBAND-REGENPFEIFER (G)**

African Snipe
Gallinago nigripennis

L 28–30cm *Dark above, with heavily streaked neck and breast and contrasting white belly.* In flight, outer tail partly barred and pale fringes to greater coverts contrast with darker wings. Wings are short and broad and bill is long. Very erratic flight when flushed. Found in marshes and flooded grassland. Fairly common resident and local nomad in wetland areas of northern Namibia. Call is a sucking 'scaap' when flushed; males make whirring, drumming sound with their stiffened outer-tail feathers in aerial display flights. **AFRIKAANSE SNIP (A) AFRIKANISCHE BEKASSINE (G)**

Common Whimbrel
Numenius phaeopus

L 40–45cm The only common large wader in Namibia with a *decurved bill. Identified by parallel pale and dark stripes on the head, bisected by a pale stripe down the centre of the crown, and by the pale eye-stripe.* In flight, tail has dusky brown bars. Imm. resembles ad. Emits a staccato, whistled call when flushed. A common summer visitor, seldom seen outside estuaries and bays; rare during winter. **KLEINWULP (A) REGENBRACHVOGEL (G)**

M. BOOYSEN

Bar-tailed Godwit   *Limosa lapponica*

L 37–40cm A large wader, with a *very long, slightly upturned bill, the basal half of which is pink. Upperparts are mottled grey and brown.* In flight, shows a white rump and fine barring on the tail. In br. plumage head, neck and underparts are rich chestnut. Imm. resembles non-br. ad. Usually silent, but does utter a 'wik-wik' call. A common summer visitor that frequents large estuaries, coastal lagoons and mud-edged lakes.
BANDSTERTGRIET (A) AMERIKANISCHE UFERSCHNEPFE (G)

Common Greenshank
Tringa nebularia

L 30–34cm A medium-sized, *pale grey wader with greyish-olive legs. Upturned black bill with a grey base* differentiates it from other waders. In flight, shows a conspicuous white rump that extends up the back into a white wedge. Imm. similar to ad. Call is a loud, rasping 'chew-chew-chew'. Often seen in the shallows chasing fish in a wide range of salt and freshwater wetlands. A common summer visitor, with a few birds remaining throughout the year.
GROENPOOTRUITER (A) GRÜNSCHENKEL (G)

Marsh Sandpiper   *Tringa stagnatilis*

L 22–26cm A *medium-sized, pale grey wader.* Smaller and more slender than Common Greenshank, with much *thinner, straight black bill and proportionally longer legs;* toes extend further beyond tail tip in flight. Rather plain upperwing contrasts with white rump and back in flight. Br. ad. has blackish mottling on upperparts. Juv. darker and browner above with buff-edged back feathers. Gives a high-pitched 'yeup'. Fairly common Palearctic migrant at freshwater and coastal wetlands.
MOERASRUITER (A) TEICHWASSERLÄUFER (G)

Wood Sandpiper
Tringa glareola

L 19–21cm Similar in size to the Common Sandpiper, but lacks the white shoulder and wing bar. Identifiable by its *brownish back, well spotted with buff or white, white rump, pale grey underwing and greenish-yellow legs.* Barred tail is visible in flight. Imm. resembles ad. but is warmer brown above. A very vocal species with a high-pitched, slightly descending 'chiff-iff-iff' call. A common summer visitor to dams, vleis, bays and estuaries. **BOSRUITER (A) BRUCHWASSERLÄUFER (G)**

Common Sandpiper
Actitis hypoleucos

L 19–21cm A small, usually solitary wader. *Uniformly brown, showing a white shoulder in front of the closed wing,* and having dull green legs. In flight, has prominent pale wing bar and barred sides to dark tail. Has a peculiar habit of bobbing backwards and forwards between short bursts of running. Imm. resembles ad. Flight call is a characteristic 'ti-ti-ti'. Occurs commonly during summer in a wide range of Namibian wetlands. **GEWONE RUITER (A) FLUSSUFERLÄUFER (G)**

Ruff
Philomachus pugnax

L ♂=20–30cm, ♀=24cm *Scaling on the upperparts* is conspicuous in this species. Leg colour highly variable, often orange or reddish; the black bill may also show an orange or reddish base. In flight, *oval white patch on either side of the rump* is diagnostic. During non-br. season the male may show a white head and neck. Imm. resembles non-br. ad. Mostly silent in Namibia. A common summer visitor to estuaries, bays and adjacent grassy areas. **KEMPHAAN (A) KAMPFLÄUFER (G)**

Ruddy Turnstone
Arenaria interpres

L 21–25cm Stocky wader with a *short, slightly flattened and upturned black bill. Legs are orange with darker joints.* In flight, upperparts show distinctive dark and light pattern. In br. plumage head and neck have clear black-and-white pattern, and wings and back are chestnut. Imm. has browner underparts, which are more heavily scaled. Gives a hard 'kttuck' call, especially in flight. A common summer visitor to the coast; some birds overwinter. **STEENLOPER (A) STEINWÄLZER (G)**

Red Knot
Calidris canutus

L 23–25cm A short-legged, plain, dumpy wader. Differs from the similar Curlew Sandpiper in being larger and having a *straight bill and greenish legs.* In flight, shows pale wing bar and rump flecked with grey. In br. plumage underparts deep chestnut, except for underwing. Imm. slightly browner than ad. Gives a nondescript 'knut' call. Gregarious wader in estuaries and bays. Common summer visitor. **KNOET (A) KNUTT (G)**

Sanderling
Calidris alba

L 19–21cm In non-br. plumage it is the *palest sandpiper in the region. Has a short, stubby black bill and a dark shoulder.* In br. plumage has black wing and back feathers with rufous centres and a broad, diffuse chestnut breast band streaked with black. In flight, shows a distinct white wing bar. Imm. resembles non-br. ad. Call is a single, decisive 'wick'. Common to abundant on the coast, although individuals sometimes found inland. **DRIETOONSTRANDLOPER (A) SANDERLING (G)**

Curlew Sandpiper
Calidris ferruginea

L 18–23cm *Small, long-legged wader with a long, obviously decurved bill.* Appears grey, with a squarish white rump, variably scalloped with pale grey. In br. plumage underparts and face become rust-coloured and rump is finely barred. Male is brighter than female. Imm. has buffy edges to mantle feathers. Gives short trill 'chirrup'. Common to abundant summer visitor that feeds in a variety of inland wetlands and coastal estuaries. **KROMBEKSTRANDLOPER (A) SICHELSTRANDLÄUFER (G)**

Little Stint
Calidris minuta

L 12–15cm A tiny wader easily identified by its small size; is invariably the smallest when seen foraging in a flock of shorebirds. Has typically nervous, rapid feeding action. In flight *narrow white wing bar and white sides to the rump* are obvious. In br. plumage head and neck become suffused with a rich russet. Gives a short, repeated 'teet' call. A common summer visitor to inland and coastal wetlands in the region. **KLEINSTRANDLOPER (A) ZWERGSTRANDLÄUFER (G)**

Red-necked Phalarope
Phalaropus lobatus

L 17–20cm In br. plumage acquires a *small chestnut gorget on the upper neck and is darker overall.* Has a *dark grey back, streaked with white, and a thin, all-black bill.* Rump is black fringed with white. Imm. similar to non-br. ad. Emits a low 'tchick' when put to flight. Found on salt pans and on quiet water bodies. An uncommon summer visitor to Namibian coastal regions; probably more common at sea. **ROOIHALSFRAIINGPOOT (A) ODINSHÜHNCHEN (G)**

Subantarctic Skua
Catharacta antarctica

L 60–66cm A large, *heavy-bodied skua with large white wing flashes* (reduced in juv.). Short, broad wings, short rump and tail and heavy build distinguish it from jaegers. Upperparts variably streaked and blotched buff; plainer in the juv. *C. a. lonnbergi* is the most frequent visitor. Generally silent at sea but does give short 'kwaark' notes. Not uncommon in shelf waters. Regular scavenger behind offshore trawlers.
BRUINROOFMEEU (A) SKUA (G)

Pomarine Jaeger
Stercorarius pomarinus

L 50cm (to 75cm with streamers) Has fairly broad wings and large white wing flashes. Heavily built, with barrel chest and stout, pale-based bill. Flight direct and powerful. Br. ad. has *spoon-shaped (not pointed) central tail feathers*. Pale morph predominates; has more extensive dark cap than other pale-morph jaegers. Non-br. ad. is barred on vent, flanks and rump. Juv. and imm. boldly barred on belly, vent, rump and underwing. Common Palearctic migrant to coastal waters off Namibia.
KNOPSTERTROOFMEEU (A) SPATELRAUBMÖWE (G)

M. TILLETT/WIKIMEDIA/CC BY 2.0

Parasitic Jaeger
Stercorarius parasiticus

L 46cm (to 65cm with streamers) *Medium-sized with white wing flashes*; usually the most abundant jaeger in Namibia. *Larger and darker* than Long-tailed Jaeger, with broader wings and more prominent white wing flashes. Smaller and more slender than Pomarine, with longer, narrower wings, smaller bill that appears uniformly dark and smaller dark hood in pale morph birds. If present, central tail feathers are relatively short and straight. **ARKTIESE ROOFMEEU (A) SCHMAROTZERRAUBMÖWE (G)**

ANDREAS TREPTE/PHOTO-NATUR.NET

pale morph

non-br.

Long-tailed Jaeger
Stercorarius longicaudus

L 38cm (to 62cm with streamers) Flight is buoyant, on long slender wings. Most are pale morphs. Ad. *cold greyish above; shafts of outer two primaries white;* vent and uppertail coverts barred in non-br. ad. *Long central tail feathers* diagnostic in br. ad. (beware short streamers when moulting). Juv. colder grey-brown than juv. Parasitic Jaeger, with more boldly barred uppertail coverts and underwing. Fairly common Palearctic migrant to oceanic waters off Namibia; scarce close to land.
LANGSTERTROOFMEEU (A) FALKENRAUBMÖWE (G)

imm.

Kelp Gull
Larus domicanus

L 55–65cm The largest gull in Namibia; easily identified by its *contrasting white body and jet black back and upperwings,* bright yellow, orange-tipped bill and greenish legs. Imm. is a very dark mottled brown, becoming paler with age. Gives a loud 'ki-ok'call and, in alarm, a short, repeated 'kwok'. Common along coastal strip and forages in the coastal zone. **KELPMEEU (A) DOMINIKANERMÖWE (G)**

non-br.

Sabine's Gull
Xema sabini

L 27–32cm *Upperwing pattern of black, white and grey triangular patches* is diagnostic in this small oceanic gull. *Small black bar crosses hindneck.* Has black bill with yellow tip; *tail is slightly forked.* Br. ad. rarely seen in region, but has jet-black hood. Occurs in small foraging flocks over the deep ocean. Sometimes blown into shallower waters and bays. Usually silent in the region. Summer visitor to the Benguela system off Namibia.
MIKSTERTMEEU (A) SCHWALBENMÖWE (G)

br.

Grey-headed Gull
Chroicocephalus cirrocephalus

L 40–42cm Ad. has diagnostic *pale grey head (darker in br. season)*. Has long bright red bill and legs. Eyes pale silver-yellow, with narrow red outer ring. In flight, outer primaries are mostly black and underwing is grey. Imm. has extensive dark-smudged ear coverts and dark-tipped, pink-orange bill. Juv. is heavily mottled brown above. Call is typical small gull's 'karrh' and 'pok-pok'. Open coast and coastal and freshwater wetlands. Locally common.
GRYSKOPMEEU (A) GRAUKOPFMÖWE (G)

imm.

Hartlaub's Gull
Chroicocephalus hartlaubii

L 38–40cm A small gull with a *dark red bill, deeper red legs and dark eye*. In br. plumage shows the suggestion of a grey hood. In non-br. plumage head is plain white. Imm. has faint brown markings on head, a brown bill, and the black tip to the tail is either reduced or absent. Gives drawn-out, rattling 'karrh' and 'pok-pok' call. Near-endemic to coastline and offshore islands of Namibia. **HARTLAUBMEEU (A)**
HARTLAUBSMÖWE (G)

imm.

Caspian Tern
Hydroprogne caspia

L 47–54cm The largest tern in southern Africa, immediately recognised by its *orange-red bill, which is usually tipped with black*. In br. ad. cap is streaked black and white; non-br. ad. has totally black cap. Imm. has an orange bill with more extensive black tip and dark-edged back feathers. Gives a loud, harsh 'kraaak' call. Found in the vicinity of large rivers, lagoons, estuaries, bays, islands and inshore waters. Uncommon on the coast.
REUSESTERRETJIE (A) RAUBSEESCHWALBE (G)

M. BOOYSEN

Swift Tern
Thalasseus bergii

L 46–49cm In *br. plumage shows white forehead*, as *black cap does not extend to the bill*. In non-br. plumage forehead and crown appear mostly white, grizzled with variable amounts of black. Has a large yellow or greenish-yellow bill. Imm. has blackish-brown barred back and tail and a dusky, yellow-olive bill. Gives a 'kee-eck' call; imm. gives a thin, vibrating whistle. Occurs in inshore waters, larger bays and estuaries, and is common along the coastal strip. **GEELBEKSTERRETJIE (A) EILSEESCHWALBE (G)**

Sandwich Tern
Thalasseus sandvicensis

L 36–40cm Large (but smaller than Swift Tern), *very pale tern* with a diagnostic *slender, yellow-tipped black bill*. In flight, shows a white rump and forked tail. Legs and feet are black. In br. plumage breast may show faint rosy hue and the cap is black. Imm. resembles non-br. ad. but has mottled upperparts. Call is a loud, grating 'kirik'. A common summer visitor found in inshore waters, estuaries and bays. **GROOTSTERRETJIE (A) BRANDSEESCHWALBE (G)**

Common Tern
Sterna hirundo

L 31–35cm The most abundant small tern on the Namibian coast in summer. Has grey upperparts, white underparts and a partially developed black cap, all features common to most small non-br. terns. The *long, slightly decurved bill and uniform grey rump* aid identification. In br. plumage, shows a black cap and pale grey underparts, a long, forked tail and a black-tipped red bill. Found on the open sea, coastal lakes and beaches. **GEWONE STERRETJIE (A) FLUSSSEESCHWALBE (G)**

Damara Tern   *Sternula balaenarum*

L 21–23cm *A small tern with a long, slightly decurved bill and uniform pale grey upperparts, rump and uppertail.* In br. plumage shows completely black cap, black bill and black legs. Imm. has brown barring on the upperparts. Gives high-pitched 'tsit-tsit' and harsh, rapid 'kid-ick' calls. Frequents sandy coasts and sheltered bays and lagoons. A common summer visitor to the coastal strip; a few birds remain throughout the year. **DAMARASTERRETJIE (A) DAMARASEESCHWALBE (G)**

Whiskered Tern   *Chlidonias hybrida*

L 25–26cm *In br. plumage dark grey (not black) underparts are diagnostic.* Non-br. ad. lacks dark cheek patch extending below eye. Rump pale grey (not white, as in White-winged Tern). Paler overall than Black Tern and lacks dark shoulder smudge. Juv. has mottled brown back. Call is a repeated, hard 'zizz' and 'krrkk'. Found at most wetlands and marshes, but requires floating vegetation to breed. Fairly common resident and Palearctic migrant. **WITBAARDSTERRETJIE (A) WEISSBART-SEESCHWALBE (G)**

White-winged Tern
Chlidonias leucopterus

L 20–22cm The most abundant small freshwater tern in the area. In br. plumage has *black underwings, paler upperwings and a pale rump and tail.* In non-br. plumage ad. is *pale grey and white, with small amounts of black on the head and underwing.* Imm. is similar to non-br. ad. Call is a short 'kek-kek'. Occurs mostly in freshwater areas, but is also found on big estuaries. **WITVLERKSTERRETJIE (A) WEISSFLÜGEL-SEESCHWALB (G)**

non-br. I SINCLAIR

Black Tern

Chlidonias niger

L 22–24cm In br. plumage, *black head, breast and belly merge into dark grey back and wings*; lacks contrast of White-winged Tern. Non-br. birds have *dark shoulder smudges*, more black on head than White-winged Tern, and no contrast between back, rump and tail. Darker than Whiskered Tern, with different head pattern. Juv. slightly darker and less uniform above. Usually silent in Africa; quiet 'kik-kik' flight call. Open ocean and coast; forages at sea, but many roost ashore. Common Palearctic migrant, mostly Aug-Apr. **SWARTSTERRETJIE (A) TRAUERSEESCHWALBE (G)**

♂

Namaqua Sandgrouse

Pterocles namaqua

L 24–28cm The only sandgrouse in the region with a *long, pointed tail*. Male has buff-spotted back and a white-and-chestnut breast band. Female is cryptically mottled and streaked with buff and brown. Imm. similar to imm. Double-banded Sandgrouse, but is more buffy yellow on the throat and breast and shows the pointed tail. In flight, gives a nasal 'kalke-ven' call, revealing its presence. Common in grasslands, desert and semi-desert. **KELKIEWYN (A) NAMAFLUGHUHN (G)**

♀

Yellow-throated Sandgrouse

Pterocles gutturalis

L 28–30cm Africa's largest sandgrouse, identified in flight by its *short tail and dark brown belly and underwings*. Male has a *creamy yellow face and throat, with a broad black neck collar*. Female heavily mottled on neck, breast and upperparts. Flight call a deep 'aw-aw', the first note higher pitched; sometimes preceded by 'ipi'. In grassland and arid savanna; drinks in the morning. Uncommon resident and seasonal visitor in northeastern Namibia. **GEELKEELSANDPATRYS (A) GELBKEHL-FLUGHUHN (G)**

♀

♂ W. TARBOTON (MAIN IMAGE)

Double-banded Sandgrouse
Pterocles bicinctus

L 25–26cm Similar to Namaqua Sandgrouse. *Male easily identified by the thin black-and-white breast band and the black and white markings on the head.* Female and imm. have a darker streaked crown, barred upper breast and short round tail. Gives a soft whistling 'chwee-chee-chee' call. Frequents woodland and savanna areas. Flocks tend to gather at waterholes just after sunset, sometimes in large numbers. **DUBBELBANDSANDPATRYS (A) NACHTFLUGHUHN G)**

Burchell's Sandgrouse
Pterocles burchelli

L 24–26cm A small sandgrouse easily identified by the combination of its *white-spotted cinnamon breast and belly, and its white-spotted back and wing coverts.* Female and imm. resemble the male but lack the blue-grey throat and are duller in colour. Gives a soft, mellow 'chup-chup, choop-choop' call in flight and when visiting waterholes midmorning. Common on red Kalahari sands. **GEVLEKTE SANDPATRYS (A) FLECKENFLUGHUHN (G)**

Speckled (Rock) Pigeon
Columba guinea

L 33cm At close range the *white-speckled, reddish back and wings, black bill, red legs and bare red skin around the eye* are diagnostic. Imm. lacks red on the face. Gives a very owl-like, deep, resonant 'hoo-hoo' call. Inhabits mountain ranges, rocky terrain and coastal cliffs. Has also adapted to urban life and is often seen on the ledges of buildings in cities. Common throughout most of Namibia, except in dense woodlands. **KRANSDUIF (A) GUINEATAUBE (G)**

P RYAN (INSET)

A. FRONEMAN/IMAGES OF AFRICA

African Mourning Dove
Streptopelia decipiens

L 28–30cm A fairly large, collared dove with a *plain grey head and broad red eye-ring contrasting with the pale yellow eye.* Smaller and paler than Red-eyed Dove, but larger than all other collared doves. In flight, has white in outer tail. Juv. browner. Calls include a loud 'cuck-ook-oooo', a grating 'currrrrrrow' and a throaty 'aaooow' on landing. Locally common resident in northern semi-arid savanna. **ROOIOOGTORTELDUIF (A) BRILLENTAUBE (G)**

Red-eyed Dove
Streptopelia semitorquata

L 32–34cm The largest collared dove; *overall dark pinkish-grey with a pale face and pinkish head and breast.* In flight has diagnostic *broad buffy band at tip of tail.* Dull red eye-ring is less prominent than that of African Mourning Dove. Juv. is browner, with smaller collar. The 'coo coo, co-kuk coo coo', call is diagnostic; also gives harsh 'chwaa' alarm call. Common resident of woodland, forest and gardens. Males fly up steeply in towering display, clapping wings, then glide back to perch in a tree. **GROOTRINGDUIF (A) HALBMONDTAUBE (G)**

P. RYAN, A. FRONEMAN/IMAGES OF AFRICA (INSET)

Cape Turtle Dove
Streptopelia capicola

L 25–27cm Probably the most abundant dove in Namibia. Shows a diagnostic *white-tipped tail* that is conspicuous in flight. Has a pale head, dark eye and black hind collar. Imm. resembles ad., but is duller and lacks hind collar. Its three-noted 'kuk-cooo-kuk' call is a familiar background sound in the bushveld. Found in virtually every habitat in the region but avoids extreme desert zones. **GEWONE TORTELDUIF (A) KAPTURTELTAUBE (G)**

Laughing Dove
Streptopelia senegalensis

L 22–24cm Similar to the larger Cape Turtle Dove but lacks the black hind collar. Also differs in having a *black-speckled necklace across its cinnamon breast and a cinnamon-coloured back*. Blue-grey forewings and white tip and sides of the tail are obvious in flight. Female smaller and paler than male; imm. duller than ad. Its name is derived from the chortled 'ooo-coooc-coooc-coo-coo' call. Frequents a wide range of habitats, avoiding extremely arid areas.
ROOIBORSDUIFIE (A) SENEGALTAUBE (G)

African Green Pigeon
Treron calvus

L 25–28cm A distinctive *parrot-like pigeon often seen clambering (parrot-like)* in the canopy of fruiting trees, especially figs. *Green, yellow and grey plumage* is unique in local pigeons. Call is a long series of liquid whistles. Locally common and nomadic in the woodlands of northern Namibia, especially at fruiting fig trees. **PAPEGAAIDUIF (A) GRÜNE FRUCHTTAUBE (G)**

M. BOOYSEN

Emerald-spotted Wood-Dove
Turtur chalcospilos

L 17–20cm *A small, compact dove with mainly plain pinkish-brown plumage, relieved by pale grey crown, 6–8 iridescent green wing coverts and dark grey bars across the back*. Juv. is browner, barred buff above. Call is a long series of muffled notes, starting hesitantly and descending in pitch at the end: 'hu, hu-hu HOO, hu-hu HOO-oo, hu-HOO, hu, hu, hu-hu-hu-hu-hu-hu-hu-hu'. Common resident in woodland and savanna; generally in drier habitats.
GROENVLEKDUIFIE (A) BRONZEFLECKTAUBE (G)

Namaqua Dove   *Oena capensis*

L 28cm The smallest-bodied dove in Namibia, and the only one in southern Africa with a *long pointed tail*. Male has a black face and throat. In flight white underparts, chestnut flight feathers and long tail render this bird unmistakable. Imm. and female lack black face of the male and have slightly shorter, pointed tail. Call is a soft, low 'coooo-hoooo'. Favours drier regions, such as thornveld, scrub and true desert, and is common in Namibia, except in the moist northern regions. **NAMAKWADUIFIE (A) KAPTÄUBCHEN (G)**

Rosy-faced Lovebird
Agapornis roseicollis

L 15–18cm Small; very well camouflaged when motionless among green foliage. Is usually detected only by its typical parrot-like screeches and shrieks. Rapid flight, with *blue rump showing up clearly against the green back*. Imm. paler on face and upper breast than ad. Breeds colonially, utilising natural cavities and crevices on cliff faces. Has also adapted to br. under eaves of houses. Near-endemic; common in mountainous terrain, dry broadleaved woodland and semi-desert regions. **ROOIWANGPARKIET (A) ROSENPAPAGEI (G)**

Meyer's Parrot   *Poicephalus meyeri*

L 21–23cm The most widespread of the brown parrots in the north. Most likely to be confused with Rüppell's Parrot in Namibia. *Rather dark brown with conspicuous blue-green rump, yellow wrists, green belly and bluish vent*. Dark bill and eye; some birds have yellow bar across crown. Juv. duller and lacks yellow on crown. Call is a loud, piercing 'chee-chee-chee-chee' with various other screeches and squawks. Found in broadleaved woodland and savanna. Scarce to locally common. **BOSVELDPAPEGAAI (A) GOLDBUGPAPAGEI (G)**

M BOYSEN

Rüppell's Parrot *Poicephalus rueppellii*

L 21–24cm Small parrot with a *greyish throat and head and blue belly*. In flight male's brown rump is very obvious. Female brighter than male, with more extensive blue on the vent and blue (not brown) rump. Imm. resembles ad. but is duller. Gives loud screeches and squawks, accompanied by piercing whistles. Near-endemic to the region. Thinly distributed through dry woodland, thornveld and dry rivercourses in northern Namibia.
BLOUPENSPAPEGAAI (A) RÜPPELLPAPAGEI (G)

Schalow's Turaco *Tauraco schalowi*

L 40–45cm A green turaco with *a long, white-tipped crest (especially at front of crest)*, dark blue or purple tail and pale green underparts. Juv. has shorter crest. Gives raucous 'kaaa kaaa' notes typical of a turaco. Uncommon, localised resident and nomad in the dense riparian woodland of northeastern Namibia.
LANGKUIFLOERIE (A) SCHALOW-TURAKO (G)

AGAMI PHOTO AGENCY/SHUTTERSTOCK.COM

Grey Go-Away-Bird
Corythaixoides concolor

L 48–50cm A conspicuous, *uniformly grey bird with long tail and crest*. Resembles a giant mousebird. Flight is strong; flapping alternates with gliding. Imm. buffier than the ad., with a shorter crest. When uttering its harsh, nasal 'waaaay' or 'kay-waaaay' call, raises its crest and flicks its tail. Occurs in thornveld and dry open woodland, and is often seen in small groups perched on top of thorn trees. **KWÊVOËL (A) GRAULÄRMVOGEL (G)**

Common Cuckoo   *Cuculus canorus*

L 32–34cm Differs from African Cuckoo in *having spotted (not barred) outer tail, more boldly barred vent and undertail coverts,* and generally less yellow at base of bill. Female has rare hepatic morph, barred black and rufous above. Juv. may be brown, grey or chestnut; upperparts usually barred, but with plain rump; underparts heavily barred. Generally silent in Africa. Frequents woodland, savanna, riverine forests and suburban gardens. Scarce to locally common Palearctic migrant Aug–Apr. **EUROPESE KOEKOEK (A) KUCKUCK (G)**

African Cuckoo   *Cuculus gularis*

L 32–34cm A large grey cuckoo. Similar to Common Cuckoo. *Ad. typically has more extensive yellow base to bill, barred (not spotted) outer tail and more finely barred vent and undertail coverts.* Call is most distinctive feature. Lacks hepatic morph. Juv. is barred black-and-white, with upperparts and rump blackish, scalloped with white (rump is plain in Common Cuckoo). Call very similar to African Hoopoe's 'hoop-hoop', but slower; female utters fast 'kik-kik-kik'. Locally common intra-African migrant in woodland and savanna. **AFRIKAANSE KOEKOEK (A) AFRIKANISCHER KUCKUCK (G)**

Black Cuckoo   *Cuculus clamosus*

L 30cm The *only all-black cuckoo in* Namibia. More often heard than seen. When observed in the canopy it may be confused with its host, the Fork-tailed Drongo, but lacks the forked tail. Imm. is duller black than ad. and has a shorter tail. Frequently repeated call is a mournful, droning 'whooo-wheeee'. A common summer visitor to shrub-and-tree savanna and woodlands throughout Namibia. **SWARTKOEKOEK (A) SCHWARZKUCKUCK (G)**

Levaillant's Cuckoo
Oxylophus levaillantii

L 38–40cm Large, *black-and-white cuckoo, with a long crest.* Larger than Jacobin Cuckoo, with *striped throat and breast.* Rare black morph differs from dark morph Jacobin in having white tail tips. Morphs have white wing patches. Juv. is browner above and buff below, but shows the distinctive throat striping. Call is a loud 'klee-klee-kleeuu', followed by descending 'che-che-che-che'. Locally common intra-African migrant in savanna and woodland. **GESTREEPTE NUWEJAARSVOËL (A) KAPKUCKUCK (G)**

Jacobin Cuckoo   *Oxylophus jacobinus*

L 33–34cm *Smaller than Levaillant's Cuckoo, with no stripes on throat and breast.* Dark morph is black, with white wing patch; smaller than dark morph Levaillant's, with no white in tail. The crest and long, graduated tail separate it from Black Cuckoo. Juv. browner above, with creamy-grey underparts; dark morph has dull black underparts. Gives a shrill repeated 'klee-klee-kleeuu-kleeuu' similar to start of Levaillant's call. In woodland, thickets and acacia savanna. Common intra-African migrant. **BONTNUWEJAARSVOËL (A) JAKOBINERKUCKUCK (G)**

M. BOOYSEN

Diederik Cuckoo   *Chrysococcyx caprius*

L 17–20cm It can be distinguished by the contrasting *bottle-green and white plumage, broad white eye-stripe, white spots on the forewing and red eye.* Imm. has a conspicuous red bill. During the summer the 'dee-dee-dee-deederic' call is heard around the colonies of the weavers and bishops that these birds parasitise. This common summer visitor occurs in open grasslands with stands of trees, in thornveld and suburbia, avoiding extreme arid regions. **DIEDERIKKIE (A) DIDERIKKUCKUCK (G)**

N. DENNIS/IMAGES OF AFRICA

Klaas's Cuckoo   *Chrysococcyx klaas*

L16–18cm Plain, *glossy green, with a small white stripe behind eye; lacks white wing spots of Diederik Cuckoo.* Male white below, with green spurs on sides of breast, and a few green bars on thighs. Female bronzy brown above, finely barred below; extent of barring varies geographically. Juv. is barred bronze and green above, and has a white eye-stripe. Gives far-carrying 'hueejee' call 3–6 times. Common intra-African migrant in woodland, savanna and gardens. **MEITJIE (A) KLAASKUCKUCK (G)**

Coppery-tailed Coucal
Centropus cupreicaudus

L 46–52cm A very large coucal with *coppery-blue sheen on head and finely barred uppertail coverts.* Much larger than White-browed or Senegal coucal, and in flight has distinct brown trailing edge to wing. Juv. is duller and more barred above. Call is a deep, loud, resonant series of 'doo' notes. Found in various marshlands, thick reedbeds and adjoining bush. Common in permanent wetlands of northern Namibia. **GROOTVLEILOERIE (A) ANGOLA-MÖNCHSKUCKUCK (G)**

White-browed Coucal
Centropus superciliosus

L 41cm A medium-sized coucal with a diagnostic *white supercilium and heavily streaked nape and mantle in ad. plumage.* Ad. has plain, not barred wings and generally is white below. Juv. is buffier than ad., with less prominent buff supercilium and barred wings. Call is a liquid, bubbling 'doo-doo-doo-doo', falling in pitch, then slowing and rising in pitch at the end. Found in reedbeds and thickets, usually close to water. Fairly common in the north. **GESTREEPTE VLEILOERIE (A) WEISSBRAUEN-SPORNKUCKUCK (G)**

M BOOYSEN

Senegal Coucal
Centropus senegalensis

L 38–40cm *A small black-capped coucal.* Much smaller than Coppery-tailed Coucal, with rich chestnut mantle and wings; lacks a bluish sheen to head. Juv. is buffy, heavily barred above. Rare rufous morph has rufous underparts. Call is a series of descending bubbling notes. Uncommon to locally common resident or partial migrant, found in tangled vegetation and long grass; less tied to water than most other coucals. **SENEGALVLEILOERIE (A) SENEGAL-SPORNKUCKUCK (G)**

African Wood Owl   *Strix woodfordii*

L 34cm *A medium-sized owl with a rounded head lacking ear tufts, dark eyes and yellow bill.* Facial disc is finely barred and paler than white-spotted brown head and upper breast; belly is barred brown and white. Larger than owlets, and lacks ear tufts of eagle-owls. Plumage varies from very dark brown to russet. Female calls 'hu hu, hu whoo-oo', to which male normally responds with a low hoot; also gives high-pitched 'who-uuu'. Occurs in evergreen and riverine forests, mature woodland and suburbia. Common. **BOSUIL (A) WOODFORDKAUZ (G)**

Southern White-faced Owl
Ptilopsis granti

L 25–28cm Differs from the smaller African Scops Owl in having a *white facial disc edged with black, paler grey plumage and bright orange (not yellow) eyes.* White-faced and African Scops owls are the only small owls to show ear tufts. Imm. is buffier than ad., with a greyish face and yellow (not orange) eyes. Call is a fast, hooting 'doo-doo-doo-doo-hohoo'. Occurs singly or in pairs in thornveld and dry broadleaved woodland. More thinly distributed than African Scops Owl, but is less well concealed. **WITWANGUIL (A) WEISSGESICHT-OHREULE (G)**

M. BOOYSEN

A. RILEY/ROCKJUMPER BIRDING TOURS

M. BODYSEN

Pearl-spotted Owlet
Glaucidium perlatum

L 17–21cm Smallest owl in the region. Head is rounded and lacks ear tufts. Has *white spotting on its tail and back,* unlike African Scops and White-faced owls. It shows *two black eye-like spots on the nape.* Imm. resembles ad. Call is a series of 'tu-tu-tu-tu' whistles, rising and descending; regularly calls during the day. Common in dry thornveld and broadleaved woodland, but may be found in suitable habitat throughout the region, except in the south. **WITKOLUIL (A) PERLKAUZ (G)**

African Scops Owl
Otus senegalensis

L 20cm Diminutive and inconspicuous. Has ear tufts like White-faced Owl. However, *its tiny size and grey (not white) face* should distinguish it. Has *greyish, bark-like plumage, yellow eyes and long ear tufts.* Although it is seldom seen, its soft frog-like 'prrrup' is often heard at night. Imm. resembles ad. Roosts by day, when it compresses its body, huddles against a trunk and slits its eyes, making it almost impossible to detect. Common in riverine forest and dry open tree savanna. **SKOPSUIL (A) AFRIKANISCHE ZWERGOHREULE (B)**

Verreaux's Eagle-Owl
Bubo lacteus

L 58–66cm A large woodland and savanna owl, easily identified by its *large size and finely vermiculated, pale grey plumage.* At close range, its pink eyelids and dark brown eyes are distinctive. Most other eagle-owls are smaller, with more boldly barred or blotched plumage; ear tufts are shorter than those of other species. Juv. is paler grey, lacking white tips to greater coverts. Call is a grunting pig-like 'unnh-unnh-unnh'. Found in broadleaved woodland, savanna, thornveld and riverine forests. Uncommon to locally common resident. **REUSE-OORUIL (A) MILCHUHU (G)**

Spotted Eagle-Owl   *Bubo africanus*

L 43–50cm The most commonly seen large owl in Namibia. Both grey and rufous colour forms occur. Has *ear tufts, yellow eyes* and *fine barring on the belly and flanks.* Imm. resembles the ad. Has adapted well to suburbia and can be seen in the evening when its 'hu-hoo' call can be heard. Common in a diverse range of habitats, from desert to mature woodland and savanna, but avoids dense forest.
GEVLEKTE OORUIL (A) FLECKENUHU (G)

Western Barn Owl   *Tyto alba*

L 30–35cm A medium-sized, *pale owl with golden-buff-and-grey upperparts, a white, heart-shaped facial disc and off-white underparts.* Little contrast between upperparts and underparts. In flight, has distinctive large head and short tail. Typical call is high-pitched 'shreeee'; also hisses and bill-clicks when disturbed. Common resident in most open habitats; avoids dense forest. Roosts in old buildings, caves, hollow trees and mine shafts. **NONNETJIE-UIL (A) SCHLEIEREULE (G)**

M. BOOYSEN

Fiery-necked Nightjar
Caprimulgus pectoralis

L 23–25cm *Dark brown, heavily marked, with a rich rufous collar, white moustache and white throat patch.* In flight, male shows *broad white outer-tail tips and small white primary patches*; creamy in female, which also has smaller tail tips. Rufous on face and breast varies. 'Good lord, deliver us' call is a familiar African night sound. Common resident and intra-African migrant in woodland and savanna throughout central and northern Namibia. Roosts on the ground under bushes. **AFRIKAANSE NAGUIL (A) ROTNACKEN-NACHTSCHWALBE (G)**

A. FRONEMAN/IMAGES OF AFRICA

R. LINDE

Rufous-cheeked Nightjar
Caprimulgus rufigena

L 22–24cm The most frequently encountered nightjar throughout most of Namibia. *Slightly smaller than Fiery-necked Nightjar with a more slender appearance, longer and narrower wings and* completely different call. Imm. resembles female. Call is a prolonged 'churring', usually preceded by a choking 'chulcoo-chukoo'. A common summer visitor and occurs widely, from arid and semi-arid areas to lightly wooded regions. **ROOIWANGNAGUIL (A) ROSTWANGEN-NACHTSCHWALBE (G)**

A. FRONEMAN/IMAGES OF AFRICA

Alpine Swift
 Tachymarptis melba

L 20–22cm A very large, brown swift with diagnostic *white belly and throat, separated by a dark breast band.* Flight is swift and direct, with deep beats of the long, scythe-like wings. Call is a shrill scream and a long, drawn-out, canary-like trill lasting about eight seconds and varying in pitch. Often seen in large, mixed flocks with other swift species. Aerial and wide ranging. Breeds on high inland cliffs with vertical cracks. Common resident and intra-African migrant.
WITPENSWINDSWAEL (A) ALPENSEGLER (G)

Bradfield's Swift
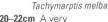 *Apus bradfieldi*

L 17cm Very similar in outline to Common Swift but paler overall and shows *scaling on breast and belly* at close range. Call is a loud and piercing 'screeee', heard at br. sites. Often associated with large palm trees where they breed, as well as in crevices on cliffs. A common Namibian near-endemic. May be encountered anywhere in the country; habitat is aerial and wide ranging.
MUISKLEURWINDSWAEL (A) DAMARASEGLER (G)

Common Swift
Apus apus

L 17cm Large congregations of swifts foraging over the bushveld in summer are usually flocks of this species. Differs from local Bradfield's Swift in being much *darker, having a more contrasting, pale throat and lacking scaling on the breast and belly.* Is usually silent in the region but will give high-pitched 'screeee' notes, especially when breeding. Habitat is aerial and wide ranging. A common summer visitor to Namibia. **EUROPESE WINDSWAEL (A) MAUERSEGLER (G)**

Little Swift
Apus affinis

L 12cm A small swift with a *large, square, white rump patch that wraps around the flanks,* and a *straight-ended (not forked) tail.* Chunkier in body than the similar White-rumped Swift, and shows a greater extent of white on the rump. In flight wing tips appear rounded. Calls include soft tittering and high-pitched screeching. Commonly seen in tight flocks over cities and towns. Usually nests colonially under the eaves of buildings, bridges and rocky overhangs. **KLEINWINDSWAEL (A) HAUSSEGLER (G)**

White-rumped Swift
Apus caffer

L 14–16cm Has a white rump and shows a diagnostic *long, deeply forked tail.* Tail usually appears *long and pointed,* as the fork is frequently held closed. Thin, 'U'-shaped white band across the rump is less obvious than in Little Swift. A swift-like scream can be heard at br. sites. A common summer visitor to the region and is frequently seen over open country and in mountainous terrain. Commonly nests under roads in concrete culverts. **WITKRUISWINDSWAEL (A) WEISSBÜRZELSEGLER (G)**

K. MORRIS

A. FRONEMAN/IMAGES OF AFRICA

African Palm Swift *Cypsiurus parvus*

L 16cm A *pale grey-brown, very slender, streamlined swift with long, thin, sickle-shaped wings and a very long, deeply forked tail*. Has the longest tail of any swift, but beware birds in moult and juvs, which have shorter, less streamer-like tails. Tail is frequently held closed and appears pointed. Call is a soft, high-pitched, twittering scream. Common resident and local migrant, usually in vicinity of palm trees, including those in towns. **PALMWINDSWAEL (A) PALMENSEGLER (G)**

White-backed Mousebird
Colius colius

L 32cm Endemic to southern Africa. Smaller, *paler and greyer* than Red-faced Mousebird, *with mostly white bill and coral pink legs*. In flight, *central back is white, bordered by glossy violet stripes (which appear black in the field)*. Paler and shorter-tailed than Red-faced Mousebird, with weaker flight. Call is a rather harsh, whistled 'zwee-wewit'. Found in scrubby areas in semi-desert. Common; usually in flocks of 3–10. **WITRUGMUISVOËL (A) WEISSRÜCKEN-MAUSVOGEL (G)**

A. FRONEMAN/IMAGES OF AFRICA

Red-faced Mousebird
Urocolius indicus

L 34cm Pale grey, with *red bill base and naked, bright red skin around the eye*. Imm. has yellowish-green face. Usually flies in small parties, either in a group or in single file. Flight action is fast and direct. Call is a diagnostic, three- or four-noted 'whee-whe-whe' whistle. Found in thornveld, open broadleaved woodland and suburban gardens. Common throughout Namibia except in extremely arid regions. **ROOIWANGMUISVOËL (A) ROTZÜGEL-MAUSVOGEL (G)**

Pied Kingfisher
Ceryle rudis

L 23–25cm The *black-and-white plumage* is unmistakable. Male has a double black breast band; female has a single, incomplete breast band. Imm. resembles female. Perches on a branch overhanging water or hovers before diving to seize a fish in its very long bill. Occasionally members in small groups interact excitedly, giving a twittering call and a sharp high-pitched 'chik-chik'. Will frequent any open stretch of fresh water, as well as coastal lagoons and wooded streams. More common in the wetter north of Namibia. **BONTVISVANGER (A) GRAUFISCHER (G)**

Malachite Kingfisher
Alcedo cristata

L 13–14cm A small aquatic kingfisher with a *diagnostic turquoise-and-black-barred crown extending down to the eye*. Ad. has all-red bill. Pale-bellied individuals occur in the north, differ greatly and may be a different species. Juv. has black bill, is blackish on back and has rufous ear coverts and diagnostic barred crown. Call is a high-pitched 'peep-peep' in flight. Found along the rivers and other freshwater bodies of permanent wetlands in northern Namibia. Common resident. **KUIFKOPVISVANGER (A) MALACHITEISVOGEL (G)**

M. BOOYSEN (MAIN IMAGE)

imm.

Woodland Kingfisher
Halcyon senegalensis

L 22–24cm Lacks the chestnut belly of similar-sized Grey-headed Kingfisher and has *greyish wash on the breast*. A black eye-stripe extends behind its eye. Juv. has dusky reddish-brown bill and is lightly barred grey on sides of breast. Call is a loud piercing 'chip-cherrrrrrrrr', descending. Found in woodland and savanna. Common resident and intra-African migrant. **BOSVELDVISVANGER (A) SENEGALLIEST (G)**

Grey-headed Kingfisher
Halcyon leucocephala

L 20–22cm *Grey head and chestnut belly* are diagnostic. Lacks any streaking on the head and flanks. Juv. has blackish bill and dark barring on breast and neck. Call is a whistled but slow 'cheeo cheeo weecho-trrrrr' and a high-pitched, rapid 'chee-chi-chi-chi-chi'; also gives a high-pitched trill. Non-aquatic and found in broadleaved woodland and savanna. Locally common resident and intra-African migrant. **GRYSKOPVISVANGER (A) GRAUKOPFLIEST (G)**

M. BODYSEN

European Bee-eater *Merops apiaster*

L 25cm (28cm incl. streamers) The only bee-eater in the region with a *chestnut crown and mantle.* In flight dazzling colours can be seen: has a *chestnut to golden back contrasting with turquoise-blue underparts and almost translucent rufous wings.* Imm. differs from ad. in having a green back and pale blue underparts. Groups in flight utter a far-carrying, policeman's whistle-like 'prrrup' call. A common summer visitor in thornveld, open, broadleaved woodland and adjacent grassy areas. **EUROPESE BYVRETER (A) EUROPÄISCHER BIENENFRESSER (G)**

A. FRONEMAN/IMAGES OF AFRICA

Blue-cheeked Bee-eater
Merops persicus

L 25cm (33cm incl. streamers) Large *green bee-eater with diagnostic green crown.* Shows blue and white cheek stripes and bluish-green breast. Juv. is duller version of the ad., with scaly upperparts. Call is a liquid 'preeo', often repeated. Found over open floodplains and adjacent woodlands, often in large foraging flocks. **BLOUWANGBYVRETER (A) BLAUWANGENSPINT (G)**

Southern Carmine Bee-eater
Merops nubicoides

L 26cm (38cm incl. streamers) *A bright red bee-eater with a black eye-stripe, turquoise crown, rump and belly and elongated, blackish central tail feathers.* Juv. duller with browner back; lacks an elongated central tail streamer. Call is a rather nasal, deep 'terk, terk' and a deep 'gra-gra-gra'. Common intra-African migrant in woodland, savanna and floodplains, chiefly in the north. Often attends grass fires. **ROOIBORSBYVRETER (A) SCHARLACHSPINT (G)**

Swallow-tailed Bee-eater
Merops hirundineus

L 20–22cm The only bee-eater in the region to have, as its name indicates, a *forked tail.* Is also identified by its yellow throat, blue collar, blue-green underparts and blue tail. Imm. *shows diagnostic forked tail, but lacks the yellow throat and blue collar.* Utters a soft twittering and calls 'kwit-kwit'. Common resident of Namibia, it frequents a diverse range of habitats from semi-desert scrub to moist evergreen forests. **SWAELSTERTBYVRETER (A) SCHWALBENSCHWANZSPINT (G)**

STEPHAN SWANEPOEL (BOTH)

Little Bee-eater
Merops pusillus

L 15–17cm *A tiny bee-eater. Has a black collar and lacks white neck stripes. Underwings are entirely russet. Central tail is green; rest of tail is russet, with black tip.* Juv. lacks black collar. Supercilium varies from green to blue. Call is a 'zeet-zeet' or 'chip-chip'. Fairly common alongside wetlands, rivers and lagoons, especially in the north. **KLEINBYVRETER (A) ZWERGSPINT (G)**

Lilac-breasted Roller
Coracias caudatus

L 29cm (37cm incl. streamers) In flight shows a range of *pale and dark blues in the wing. Lilac breast* and elongated, pointed outer-tail feathers are seen at rest. Imm. resembles ad., but lacks the long outer-tail feathers. When displaying, male utters harsh squawks and screams. Occurs in a range of habitats, from thornveld to open broadleaved woodland. Frequently seen on telephone wires and poles along roadsides. Common in the wooded and thornveld regions of Namibia.
GEWONE TROUPANT (A) GABELRACKE (G)

European Roller   *Coracias garrulus*

L 30–32cm *A large, stocky roller with a square tail lacking tail streamers.* Larger than Lilac-breasted Roller, with a bigger head and bill; flight feathers blackish (not blue) from above. Plumage can often be rather scruffy. Ad. has bluish head separated from brown back. Juv. is more olive-green, with pinkish wash on the throat; told from juv. Lilac-breasted Roller by larger head and black flight feathers. Normally silent in Africa; gives a dry 'krask-kraak' when alarmed. Common Palearctic migrant to savanna; rare in more open habitats.
EUROPESE TROUPANT (A) BLAURACKE (G)

Purple Roller   *Coracias naevius*

L 35–40cm The largest roller in southern Africa and easily identified by its *broad, pale eyebrow stripe and lilac-brown underparts streaked with white.* Imm. is duller version of the ad. In display flight it utters a harsh, repeated 'karaa-karaa' while flying with an exaggerated, side-to-side rocking motion. Found in dry thornveld and open broadleaved woodland. Common resident in Namibia, with some local movement in certain areas.
GROOTTROUPANT (A) STRICHELRACKE (G)

African Grey Hornbill
Tockus nasutus

L 44–50cm Male is only small hornbill in the region with a dark bill. Female might be confused with Southern Yellow-billed Hornbill as the upperparts of the bill are yellow in both species. *Dark head and breast and conspicuous white eyebrow stripe* aid identification. Imm. similar to male but lacks the casque. Emits a series of piping, 'phee pheeoo phee pheeoo' notes. Occurs in thornveld and dry, broadleaved woodland. Common in the region, except in true desert areas.
GRYSNEUSHORINGVOËL (A) GRAUTOKO (G)

M. BOOYSEN (BOTH)

Southern Yellow-billed Hornbill
Tockus leucomelas

L 48–60cm Resembles Damara Red-billed Hornbill in coloration but has diagnostic *large, long, yellow bill*. Might be confused with the female Grey Hornbill, which has a shorter, part-yellow bill, but is distinguished by its dark head and breast. Both imm. and female have a noticeably smaller bill and casque. Spreads its wings while giving 'tok-tok-tork-tork' notes. Frequents thornveld and broadleaved woodland and is widely but thinly distributed in the region. **GEELBEKNEUSHORINGVOËL (A) GELBSCHNABELTOKO (G)**

Bradfield's Hornbill *Tockus bradfieldi*

L 50–57cm *More uniformly brown than African Grey Hornbill, with longer, orange-red bill, no distinct casque*, no yellow line at base of bill, and red (not yellow) eye. Unlike Monteiro's Hornbill lacks white in wings and has mainly brown (not white) outer-tail feathers. Female has a smaller bill than male, with turquoise (not black) facial skin. Juv. has small bill. Gives rapidly repeated, whistling 'chleeoo' note, with bill raised vertically. Near-endemic. Fairly common resident in open mixed woodland.
BRADFIELDNEUSHORINGVOËL (A) BRADFIELDTOKO (G)

M. BOOYSEN

Monteiro's Hornbill   *Tockus monteiri*

L 50–58cm A large red-billed bird with diagnostic *white patches on the secondaries* and a *large expanse of white on outer-tail feathers*. Bradfield's Hornbill differs from this species by lacking white in the wings and having a white-tipped tail. Imm. has smaller bill. Gives hollow-sounding 'tooaaka-tooaaka' call. A common Namibian endemic, frequenting dry thornveld, well-treed, dry river beds and broadleaved woodland. **MONTEIRONEUSHORINGVOËL (A) MONTEIROTOKO (G)**

Southern Red-billed Hornbill
Tockus rufirostris

L 38–45cm Differs from Damara Red-billed Hornbill in *having brown-streaked (not white) facial feathers and pale yellow (not brown) eye*. Told from Monteiro's and Bradfield's hornbills by its white (not brown) throat, smaller bill and boldly spotted upperwing coverts. The 'kuk kuk kuk' calls get faster and louder, ending with 'kuk-we kuk-we'. Does not raise its wings during its display. Locally common in savanna and semi-arid woodland. **ROOIBEKNEUSHORINGVOËL (A) ROTSCHNABELTOKO (G)**

Damara Red-billed Hornbill
Tockus damarensis

L 40–50cm Like the Southern Red-billed Hornbill, but with a much *whiter head and neck and dark brown (not yellow) eyes*. White face, neck and breast, spotted wing coverts and smaller bill separate it from larger Monteiro's Hornbill. Gives 'kwa kwa kwa kokkok kokkok kokkok' call. Locally common in savanna and semi-arid woodland. Near-endemic to Namibia. **DAMARAROOIBEKNEUSHORINGVOËL (A) DAMARA ROTSCHNABELTOKO (G)**

GRAHAM DUGGAN

Green Wood-hoopoe
Phoeniculus purpureus

L 32–36cm Larger than Common Scimitarbill. Has a *long, decurved, red bill, red legs, white wing bars and a long white-tipped tail.* Bottle-green head and back distinguish it from the similar Violet Wood-hoopoe. Female has shorter, less decurved bill than male; imm. has black, not red, far less decurved bill. Harsh cackling call is slower than that of Violet Wood-hoopoe. Common in mixed woodland and thornveld and replaces Violet Wood-hoopoe in the northeast of the region. **ROOIBEKKAKELAAR (A) STEPPENBAUMHOP (G)**

Violet Wood-hoopoe
Phoeniculus damarensis

L 30–40cm A large wood-hoopoe with a *violet head, mantle and back*; lacks bottle-green sheen of the similar Green Wood-hoopoe. Is also larger and longer-tailed, with a more laboured and floppier flight action. Imm. resembles ad. but is duller, with a black, not red, bill. Gives harsh cackling and chattering call. A common endemic in the central and northern areas in tall thornveld, on dry rivercourses and in broadleaved woodland. **PERSKAKELAAR (A) DAMARABAUMHOPF (G)**

Common Scimitarbill
Rhinopomastus cyanomelas

L 24–28cm In flight shows white bars on the primaries, and long, graduated, white-tipped tail. Black in the field, but purple in sunlight. Has thin, very decurved, black bill. Smaller and more slender than Violet and Green Wood-hoopoes. Imm. has black, not red, legs and feet and more decurved bill than imm. Green Wood-hoopoe. Call a whistling 'sweep-sweep-sweep' and harsh chattering. Frequents thornveld and dry broadleaved woodland. **SWARTBEKKAKELAAR (A) SICHELHOPF (G)**

A. FRONEMAN/IMAGES OF AFRICA (INSET)

I. MERRILL

A. FRONEMAN/IMAGES OF AFRICA

African Hoopoe
Upupa africana

L 25–28cm Easily identified by the combination of a *cinnamon-coloured body, black-and-white-barred wings and tail, and a long decurved bill.* Female is duller than male, with less white in the wings; imm. is duller than female. Often keeps black-tipped crest closed, but holds it erect when alarmed. Frequently utters a soft 'hoop-hoop-hoop' call. Common resident in thornveld, open broadleaved woodland, parks and gardens.

HOEPHOEP (A) WIEDEHOPF (G)

Black-collared Barbet
Lybius torquatus

L 18–20cm *Bright red face and throat, broadly bordered with black.* Belly is yellow to off-white. Some races have more orange breast, and rare colour morph has a yellow face and throat. Juv's head and throat are dark brown, streaked with orange and red. Duet starts with a harsh 'krrr krrrr', followed by a ringing 'tooo puudly tooo puudly', the 'tooo' being higher pitched. Found in forests, woodland, savanna and gardens. Common in the north, often in groups. **ROOIKOPHOUTKAPPER (A) HALSBAND-BARTVOGEL (G)**

Acacia Pied Barbet
Tricholaema leucomelas

L 16–18cm The combination of a *red forehead, bright yellow eyebrow and broad white stripe behind the eye* is diagnostic. Has a black throat, white underparts and a black back with narrow yellow streaking. Imm. has black (not red) forehead. Gives a nasal 'nehh-nehh' call, repeated at intervals, or a hoopoe-like 'doo-doo-doo'. Common resident found alone or in pairs in dry broadleaved woodland, thornveld and scrub; avoids true desert.

BONTHOUTKAPPER (A) ROTSTIRN-BARTVOGEL (G)

Yellow-fronted Tinkerbird
Pogoniulus chrysoconus

L10–11cm Distinctive, with white-streaked black upperparts and yellowish underparts. *Yellow, not red, forehead and pale yellow throat* distinguish this species from the much larger Acacia Pied Barbet. Forehead *varies from pale yellow to bright orange.* Juv. lacks yellow forehead. Call is a continuous 'pop-pop-pop ...' or 'tink tink tink ...' Common in woodland and savanna. **GEELBLESTINKER (A) GELBSTIRN-BARTVOGEL (G)**

D. KEATS/WIKIMEDIA/CC BY 2.0

Lesser Honeyguide   *Indicator minor*

L 15cm Overall a dull greyish bird with an unmarked *grey head, a greenish wash on the wing coverts, dark moustachial stripes and conspicuous white outer-tail feathers.* Imm. lacks the moustachial stripes of the ad. Easily detected by its distinctive 'klew klew klew' call. Occurs in woodland, forests and thornveld, and has adapted to suburban gardens. Common resident. Often seen interacting with its brood host, the Acacia Pied Barbet. **KLEINHEUNINGWYSER (A) KLEINER HONIGANZEIGER (G)**

ALAN MANSON/CC BY-SA 3.0

Golden-tailed Woodpecker
Campethera abingoni

L 19–22cm Male has *full red crown and moustachial stripes. Streaked, not spotted, underparts* and ear coverts separate it from Bennett's Woodpecker. Back is greenish, with pale yellow bars. Female has white-spotted black crown, red nape and black-speckled moustachial stripes. Common. Call is a loud, nasal shriek, 'wheeeeeaa'. Occurs in woodland and thickets. **GOUDSTERTSPEG (A) GOLDSCHWANZSPECH (G)**

STEPHAN SWANEPOEL

Bennett's Woodpecker
Campethera bennettii

L 22–24cm Male has *full red crown and moustachial stripes and plain face and throat.* Told from male Golden-tailed Woodpecker by *white throat and spotted, not streaked, breast.* Female has *diagnostic brown throat and cheek stripe.* Sides of neck, breast and flanks spotted in nominate race, but northern Namibia *capricorni* is paler with little spotting and a yellow wash on breast. High-pitched, chattering 'whirrr-itt, whrrr-itt', often given in duet. Scarce to common in broadleaved woodland; often feeds on ground. **BENNETTSPEG (A) BENNETTSPECHT (G)**

Bearded Woodpecker
Dendropicos namaquus

L 23–25cm Much bigger than Cardinal Woodpecker. *White face, bold black moustachial stripes and black stripe through and behind the eye* are diagnostic. Underparts dark, with fine black-and-white barring. Male's hind crown and nape are red; in female they are black. Imm. has red crown and nape. Taps wood loudly and utters a loud 'kweek-eek-eek-eek'. Common resident in thornveld, riverine forests and broadleaved woodland. **BAARDSPEG (A) NAMASPECHT (G)**

Cardinal Woodpecker
Dendropicos fuscescens

L 14–16cm The smallest woodpecker in the region. Has bold *black moustachial stripes* and appears *black-and-white all over.* Male has brown forehead and a red nape; female lacks red nape. Imm. has red crown and a black nape. Sometimes difficult to locate, but its incessant soft tapping on wood and high-pitched 'krrrek-krrrek-krrrek' call reveal its position. Frequents a wide range of habitats from thornveld to thick forest. **KARDINAALSPEG (A) KARDINALSPECH (G)**

A. FRONEMAN/IMAGES OF AFRICA

Red-capped Lark *Calandrella cinerea*

L 14–15cm *Long-winged, slender, with a short bill and plain white underparts. Rufous cap and epaulettes on sides of breast* more prominent in male. Dark brown wings more pointed than those of other larks, with broad bases. Juv. dark brown above; feathers fringed with white; breast heavily spotted. Flight call is a sparrow-like 'tchweerp'. Male gives jumbled phrases in display flight. Common resident, local nomad and intra-African migrant in areas of short grass. Often in flocks. Does not require access to water. **ROOIKOPLEWERIK (A) ROTSCHEITELLERCHE (G)**

Dusky Lark *Pinarocorys nigricans*

L 19–20cm A large thrush-like lark, with a *bold black-and-white facial pattern.* When perched in trees, heavy spotting on the underparts is visible. *Characteristically raises its wings slightly above its body when walking.* Imm. has heavily mottled underparts. Utters a soft 'chrrp, chrrp' call when flushed. Occurs in open grassy areas in thornveld and broadleaved woodland, especially recently burnt areas. A regular summer visitor, but is neither common nor predictable. **DONKERLEWERIK (A) DROSSELLERCHE (G)**

Spike-heeled Lark
Chersomanes albofasciata

L 13–15cm Long-legged lark with a very upright stance. Combination of a *long, slightly decurved bill, white throat patch contrasting strongly with darker underparts,* and a *remarkably short, dark, white-tipped tail* is diagnostic. Plumage highly variable. Male is larger than female. Imm. has white mottling above and below. Can be heard giving its trilling 'trrrep, trrrep' call in flight. Common resident, occurring in sparse grassland, scrub desert and on gravel plains. **VLAKTELEWERIK (A) ZIRPLERCHE (G)**

pale morph

rufous morph

Sabota Lark   *Calendulauda sabota*

L 15cm A small nondescript lark with a *short thick bill and a straight white eye-stripe that gives it a capped appearance.* Lacks the chestnut in the outer wings seen in many similar larks. Imm. is tawnier than ad., with mottled upperparts. Sits on small trees or telephone wires, mimicking other birds and producing its jumbled song. Often found in rocky areas in dry thornveld and open broadleaved woodland. Common in Namibia, especially in Etosha.
SABOTALEWERIK (A)   SABOTALERCHE (G)

Dune Lark   *Calendulauda erythrochlamys*

L 17–18cm A sandy-coloured lark endemic to Namibia. Has a *plain or slightly streaked sandy-brown back and slightly streaked underparts.* Imm. shows pale edgings to feathers on the back. Is usually silent but sometimes gives a short, clipped song. The only true endemic of Namibia, the Dune Lark is restricted to the central Namib dune sea, and is locally common in dune and inter-dune areas with sparse grass and shrub cover. **DUINLEWERIK (A)   DÜNENLERCHE (G)**

M. BOOYSEN

Monotonous Lark   *Mirafra passerina*

L 14cm Easily overlooked when it is not singing or displaying, but when observed has an obvious *white throat contrasting with a dark streaked breast, rufous wings and white outer-tail feathers.* During the late summer and rainy season it displays conspicuously and calls from exposed perches. Gives a 'trrp-chup-chup-choop' call, repeated often during the day and at night. Very common and is found in thornveld savanna and open woodland.
BOSVELDLEWERIK (A)   SPERLINGSLERCHE (G)

A. FRONEMAN (BOTH)

display

Benguela Long-billed Lark
Certhilauda benguelensis

L 18–20cm A large elongate lark with a long decurved bill. Very *heavily streaked on the crown, back and breast.* Identification criteria require clarification. Call is a long, slightly quavering, descending 'seeoeeooooo' whistle. Occurs northwestern Namibia, but exact range is uncertain. Near-endemic common resident on arid hill slopes, ridges and gravel plains. **KAOKOLANGBEKLEWERIK (A) BENGUELA LANGSCHNABELLERCHE (G)**

Stark's Lark
Spizocorys starki

L 13–14cm Small, pale-coloured lark. At rest, shows a *pale pink bill and a streaked necklace on the breast.* When startled, raises its *long, pointed, erectile crest,* which is diagnostic. Imm. spotted white on upperparts. Dangles its long, flesh-coloured legs in display flight. Song is a short, jumbled mixture of notes. Sometimes occurs singly but is most likely to be seen in small flocks. Common but nomadic, occurring on stony desert and in grassy semi-desert areas. **WOESTYNLEWERIK (A) STARKS KURZHAUBENLERCHE (G)**

Gray's Lark
Ammomanes grayi

L 13–14cm A small endemic lark. The palest and least marked lark in the region. Plumage is *very plain, lacking streaking and barring,* hence it is unlikely to be confused with any other lark. Imm. is mottled above. Gives a short 'tseet' flight call and a ringing, metallic 'ping-ping'. Frequents coastal gravel plains and is common but thinly distributed in the region. **NAMIBLEWERIK (A) NAMIBLERCHE (G)**

Black-eared Sparrowlark
Eremopterix australis

L 12–13cm *Male black with broad chestnut margins to back, wing and tail feathers; black underwings.* Female is streaked chestnut and dark brown above, heavily streaked with black below; lacks dark belly patch of other female sparrowlarks and has black secondaries. Juv. like female, but spotted buff above. Gives short 'preep' or 'chip-chip' in flight; male has a butterfly-like aerial display. Endemic. Locally common and nomadic in Nama karoo dwarf scrub. Usually in flocks. **SWART-OORLEWERIK (A) SCHWARZWANGENLERCHE (G)**

Chestnut-backed Sparrowlark
Eremopterix leucotis

L 12–13cm *Has chestnut back and wings and black-and-white head.* Lacks white crown patch of male Grey-backed Sparrowlark; vent white, not black. Female buff-and-brown mottled, with black lower breast and belly and pale rump. Juv. like female, with pale-spotted upperparts; dark belly patch smaller or absent. Gives 'chip-chwep' call in flight. Common resident and nomad in sparse savanna and cultivated lands, favours burnt areas; usually in flocks. Often visits water to drink. **ROOIRUGLEWERIK (A) WEISSWANGENLERCHE (G)**

Grey-backed Sparrowlark
Eremopterix verticalis

L 13–14cm On the ground the diagnostic *all-black underparts, greyish upperparts and wings, and black-and-white patterned head* are clearly visible. Male has white patch on the hind crown. Female has pale conical bill and greyish upperparts, with just a patch of black on the belly. Imm. more mottled than female. Flight call 'chruk, chruk'. Mostly in small flocks in scrub, true desert and cultivated lands. Common resident, but nomadic in some areas. **GRYSRUGLEWERIK (G) NONNENLERCHE (G)**

A. FRONEMAN/IMAGES OF AFRICA (MAIN IMAGE)

Barn (European) Swallow
Hirundo rustica

L 15–20cm Identified by the diagnostic *brick red face and throat, black breast band and deeply forked tail.* Underparts are off-white to buffish. Has white spots on the tail base and long tail streamers. Male's tail longer than that of female. Imm. is browner and has shorter outer-tail feathers. Gives a soft, high-pitched twittering call. A common summer visitor, found in virtually every habitat in the region. **EUROPESE SWAEL (A) RAUCHSCHWALBE (G)**

A. FRONEMAN/IMAGES OF AFRICA

Wire-tailed Swallow
Hirundo smithii

L 12–14cm Combination of *chestnut crown and plain white underparts* is diagnostic. Juv is less glossy blue above, with a brown crown. Gives a sharp, metallic 'tchik' call; song is a twittering 'chirrik-weet, chirrik-weet'. Flight is extremely rapid. Usually found near water, often br. under bridges. Common resident in the north and an intra-African br. migrant. **DRAADSTERTSWAEL (A) ROTKAPPENSCHWALBE (G)**

P. PICKFORD/IMAGES OF AFRICA

Pearl-breasted Swallow
Hirundo dimidiata

L 13cm Small, with *off-white to white underparts and completely blue-black upperparts.* In flight, contrasting black-and-white plumage rules out confusion with other swallows. Gives a subdued chipping note, mostly in flight. Often seen perched on telephone or fence wires along roadsides, especially near road culverts where it breeds. A common but thinly distributed resident; undertakes local movements in parts of its range. **PÊRELBORSSWAEL (A) PERLBRUSTSCHWALBE (G)**

Lesser Striped Swallow
Cecropis abyssinica

L 15–17cm Smaller and darker than Greater Striped Swallow, with *heavy black (not narrow weak) striping on whiter underparts and darker, more rufous rump.* Female has shorter tail streamers than male. Juv. has less blue-black gloss above than ad. and brown (not rufous) crown. Song is a descending series of squeaky nasal 'zeh-zeh-zeh-zeh' notes. Usually found near water. An inter-African summer breeding migrant but present all year in the north. **KLEINSTREEPSWAEL (A) KLEINE STREIFENSCHWALBE (G)**

Greater Striped Swallow
Cecropis cucullata

L 16–20cm *Crown and rump are pale orange and the ear coverts are white.* At close range faint striping on the white underparts is noticeable. Imm. has small amount of blue-black gloss above; the crown is reddish-brown and the breast has a partial brown band. Call is a twittering 'chissick' and a discordant 'zzrreeeoo'. A common summer breeding migrant to the region. Found in open grassland and near vleis as well as along roadsides, especially near culverts. **GROOTSTREEPSWAEL (A) GROSSE STREIFENSCHWALBE (G)**

M. BOOYSEN

Red-breasted Swallow
Cecropis semirufa

L 20–24cm A very large, dark swallow, easily identified by its diagnostic *red throat and breast.* In flight, dark buffy underwing coverts can be seen. The remaining plumage is glossy blue-black. Imm. has creamy-white throat and breast. In flight utters a soft, warbling song with harsh twittering notes. A common summer visitor to the more northerly regions. Usually encountered in pairs along the roadside in grassland and savanna areas. **ROOIBORSSWAEL (A) ROTBAUCHSCHWALBE (G)**

Mosque Swallow
Cecropis senegalensis

L 22–26cm *Large; red-rumped; slightly larger than Red-breasted Swallow, with a white (not red) throat, face and upper breast, pale rufous (not dark blue) ear coverts and white (not buffy) underwing coverts.* Juv. duller with short tail streamers and pale buff underwing coverts, but coverts always paler than those of Red-breasted Swallow. Gives a nasal 'harrrrp' and guttural chuckling. Locally common resident in the north and a partial migrant in open woodland and especially near baobabs. **MOSKEESWAEL (A) SENEGALSCHWALBE (G)**

South African Cliff Swallow
Petrochelidon spilodera

L 14–15cm Differs from the similar Greater Striped Swallow in having only a *slight notch in the square-ended tail, a distinct breast band,* and in being *more rufous below with much reduced streaking.* Imm. lacks the blue-black gloss above. Utters indistinct 'chooerp-chooerp' call near nesting colonies. Occurs in upland grasslands, usually near road bridges under which it frequently nests. A common but unevenly distributed summer visitor. **FAMILIESWAEL (A) KLIPPENSCHWALBE (G)**

Brown-throated Martin
Riparia paludicola

L 12cm Occurs in two colour forms: one is *dark brown and shows a small amount of white on the vent;* the other, *paler form has a brown throat and breast with the remainder of the underparts white.* Dark brown form often confused with Rock Martin, but is smaller, darker brown below and lacks white tail spots. Imm. has pale fringes on the secondaries. Call is a soft twittering. Common resident; occurs over sandbanks near rivers. **AFRIKAANSE OEWERSWAEL (A) BRAUNKEHL-UFERSCHWALBE (G)**

Rock Martin
Ptyonoprogne fuligula

L 14cm A *medium-sized martin with all-brown plumage.* Could be confused with the dark form of the Brown-throated Martin, a smaller species. The Rock Martin has slightly paler underparts and, when in flight, white spots are visible on its tail. Imm. has pale edges on the upperwing coverts and secondaries. Call is a series of soft indistinct twitterings. Common resident that favours rocky, mountainous terrain but has adapted to towns and cities.
KRANSSWAEL (A) FELSENSCHWALBE (G)

Fork-tailed Drongo
Dicrurus adsimilis

L 23–26cm A noisy *all-black bird with a deeply forked tail.* Perches freely in the open, from where it hawks insects in flight or drops to the ground to retrieve food. Imm. has buff-tipped feathers on the underparts and forewing, and shows a yellow gape. Sometimes mimics the calls of birds of prey, especially those of the Pearl-spotted Owlet, and produces a variety of grating or shrill 'tchwaak tchweeek' notes. Common resident; inhabits a diverse range of habitats.
MIKSTERTBYVANGER (A) TRAUERDRONGO (G)

Black Cuckooshrike
Campephaga flava

L 18–21cm Male distinguished by *slightly glossy, all-black plumage and yellow gape.* Often shows a yellow shoulder. Female has *green-and-yellow barred plumage with bright yellow outer-tail feathers.* Imm. resembles female. Call is a high-pitched, prolonged 'trrrrrrr'. Afrotropical breeding migrant, but may be resident in broadleaved woodland in northern Namibia. **SWARTKATAKOEROE (A) KUCKUCKSWÜRGER (G)**

African Golden Oriole
Oriolus auratus

L 20–24cm A bright *golden-yellow bird, showing yellow wing coverts and a diagnostic black lozenge-shaped area around the eye*. Female similar to the male, but with duller streaking on breast and belly and has yellowish-green wing coverts. Imm. resembles female. Call is a liquid, whistled 'fee-yoo, fee-yoo'. A fairly common summer visitor to the wooded northern regions of Namibia, including miombo woodland, riverine forest and thornveld. **AFRIKAANSE WIELEWAAL (A) SCHWARZOHRPIROL (G)**

♀

♂

M. BOOYSEN, SUE ROBINSON (INSET)

Eurasian Golden Oriole
Oriolus oriolus

L 22–25cm Male is *yellow and black with black wings and black eye-stripe that extends marginally behind the eye*. Female is similar but less yellow below, with plain wing coverts (lacking yellow edges) and a less extensive dark line behind the eye. Juv is whitish below, with dark green streaks; bill is blackish. The song is a liquid 'chleeooop', but chattering sub-song and grating 'naaah' are typically heard in Namibia. Found in woodland, savanna and suburbia. Fairly common Palearctic migrant, Oct–Apr. **EUROPESE WIELEWAAL (A) EUROPÄISCHER PIROL (G)**

J.M. GARG/WIKIMEDIA/CC BY SA 3.0

Black-headed Oriole
Oriolus larvatus

L 20–24cm *The only black-headed oriole in Namibia*. Whitish edges to outer secondaries form a diagnostic pale panel in closed wing. Inner secondaries are edged yellow. Central tail feathers are olive-green above. Juv. is duller, with dark brown, slightly mottled head and dark bill. Gives explosive 'pooodleeoo' and a harsher 'kweeer'. Frequents mature, especially broadleaved woodland, forest edges and suburbia. Fairly common. **SWARTKOPWIELEWAAL (A) MASKENPIROL (G)**

M. BOOYSEN

Pied Crow
Corvus albus

L 46–50cm Very easy to identify as it is the only crow in the region with a *white belly* contrasting sharply with the otherwise black plumage. The black-and-white plumage of the imm. resembles that of the ad. but is less contrasting. Call is a loud cawing 'kwaaa' or 'kwooork'. Common resident, it often occurs in flocks and is found in virtually every habitat. Also a common city dweller, roosting in trees and regularly visiting rubbish dumps. **WITBORSKRAAI (A) SCHILDRABE (G)**

Cape Crow
Corvus capensis

L 45–50cm A *glossy black crow with a long, slender, slightly decurved bill*. The only all-black crow likely to be seen in the veld away from human habitation. Imm. is duller and lacks the glossy black plumage of ad. Gives loud, crow-like 'kah-kah' and other deep bubbling notes. Occurs in open country and cultivated fields as well as in arid regions and is often seen on roadsides in the desert. Common resident. **SWARTKRAAI (A) KAPKRÄHE (G)**

Ashy Tit
Parus cinerascens

L 15cm A small tit identified by its *slate grey body, white-fringed wings, black cap, white cheeks and a black throat and bib extending as a black line down the belly*. Imm. is a duller version of the ad. Travels in pairs or parties, keeping in contact with others in the party using a variety of ringing whistles and harsher calls. Very active and occurs in thornveld, broadleaved woodland and riverine scrub. Common resident. **AKASIAGRYSMEES (A) ASCHENMEISE (G)**

Southern Black Tit
Parus niger

L 15–16cm Within its range in Namibia, can only be confused with Carp's Tit, from which it differs in having *barred grey (not black) vent and less white in wings.* Female and juv. are paler grey below than Carp's Tit, with less white in the wings. Call is a harsh, chattering 'chrr-chrr-chrr' and a musical 'phee-cher-phee-cher'. Common in forest and broadleaved woodland, chiefly in northeastern Namibia. Usually in small groups.
GEWONE SWARTMEES (A) MOHRENMEISE (G)

Carp's Tit
Parus carpi

L 14cm Near-endemic to Namibia. Has a *black vent and very extensive white in the wings.* Male has all-black body; female is sooty grey, with a darker belly. Juv. duller than female, with yellowish fringes to flight feathers. Like many tits, gives various whistles and harsh churring notes. Fairly common resident in semi-arid savanna woodland.
OVAMBOSWARTMEES (A) RÜPPELLMEISE (G)

Black-faced Babbler
Turdoides melanops

L 24–28cm The most furtive of all the babblers. *Faint white streaking on the head, a small black patch at the base of the bill and a bright yellow eye* are diagnostic. Imm. is similar to the ad. but has a brown (not yellow) eye. Call is a nasal 'wha-wha-wha'. Shy; tends to forage in scattered groups among leaf litter. Near-endemic to Namibia. Locally common in mixed *Hyphaena* palm savanna and broadleaved woodland in the northeast. **SWARTWANGKATLAGTER (A) DUNKLER DROSSLING (G)**

Hartlaub's Babbler
Turdoides hartlaubii

L 24–26cm The *white rump, a diagnostic feature in this species, is seen in flight.* At rest it may be told from Black-faced Babbler by *its red (not yellow) eye and its paler head with white scalloping (not streaking).* The noisy 'whaaa-whaa-whaa' call is typical of babblers, with several birds often calling simultaneously. Locally common in undergrowth along the perennial rivers of northern Namibia. **WITKRUISKATLAGTER (A) WEISSBÜRZELDROSSLING (G)**

Southern Pied Babbler
Turdoides bicolor

L 23–26cm Easily identified, as it is the only babbler in the region with an *all-white head, back and underparts. Wings and tail are black.* Imm. is initially pale brown all over but lightens with age. Its typical 'kwee kwee kwee kweer' babbling call is pitched higher than that of other babblers. Conspicuous small groups fly in loose formation from bush to bush in thornveld and arid savanna. Common resident in Namibia. **WITKATLAGTER (A) ELSTERDROSSLING (G)**

A. FRIDEMAN/IMAGES OF AFRICA

Bare-cheeked Babbler
Turdoides gymnogenys

L 24–26cm The small area of *bare black skin below and behind the eye* is diagnostic. Unlike Southern Pied Babbler has a dark back and lacks white on wing coverts. Imm. much darker than imm. Southern Pied Babbler, especially on back and nape. Gives a typical babbler's 'kwee kwee kwee kweer' call. Near-endemic. Found in arid tree-and-shrub savanna in central and northwestern Namibia; favours dense vegetation along seasonal rivers and on rock outcrops. **KAAL-WANGKATLAGTER (A) NACKTOHRDROSSLING (G)**

M. BOOYSEN

African Red-eyed Bulbul
Pycnonotus nigricans

L 19cm As its name implies, has a diagnostic *red eye and eye-ring*. Its dark head contrasts with the greyish-buff collar and breast. Imm. differs from ad. in having a pale pink eye-ring. Utters a chirpy liquid 'cheloop chreep choop' call and gives a shorter 'kwit-kwit' call as an alarm note. The most common bulbul in Namibia and occurs in various habitats, including thornveld and riverine bush. Also found in more arid regions, especially around waterholes and is commonly seen in suburban gardens. **ROOIOOGTIPTOL (A) MASKENBÜLBÜL (G)**

Dark-capped Bulbul
Pycnonotus tricolor

L 19–22cm *Black (not red) eye-ring* separates it from African Red-eyed Bulbul. Also has paler underparts and more defined breast band. The alarm call is a harsh 'kwit, kwit, kwit'; the song is liquid 'sweet sweet sweet-potato'. Occurs in a wide range of habitats from savanna to forest edges and gardens. Abundant in the northeast. **SWARTOOGTIPTOL (A) GELBSTEISSBÜLBÜL (G)**

Kurrichane Thrush
Turdus libonyanus

L 21cm *A pale grey thrush with a white belly and rufous flanks*. Black speckling on the throat is concentrated into diagnostic, *broad black malar stripes*. Bill is brighter orange than those of most other African thrushes. Also has a narrow yellow eye-ring. Call is a loud whistling 'peet-peeoo'. Fairly common in moist teak woodland and gardens of northeastern Namibia. **ROOIBEKLYSTER A) ROTSCHNABELDROSSEL (G)**

Groundscraper Thrush
Psophocichla litsitsirupa

L 21–23cm Identified by the *bold contrasting facial markings and heavy spotting on the breast.* In flight a chestnut panel is visible in the wing. Imm. has speckled off-white underparts with conspicuous white-tipped wing coverts. The song is a clearly whistled 'lit-sit-si-rupa', hence its specific name. Common resident. Much bolder than other thrushes and is frequently seen hopping around in parks and gardens; also frequents thornveld and open broadleaved woodland.
GEVLEKTE LYSTER (A) AKAZIENDROSSEL (G)

Short-toed Rock Thrush
Monticola brevipes

L 16–18cm Male has a diagnostic *blue-grey crown, forehead and nape.* Crown can be so pale as to appear almost white in some individuals. Female has an extensively striped throat and breast. Imm. is spotted with buff on the upperparts and with black below. The thin whistled song includes some mimicry of other bird calls. Near-endemic to Namibia. Occurs on thickly wooded koppies and rocky slopes and is sometimes conspicuous on telephone poles. **KORTTOONKLIPLYSTER (A) KURZZEHENRÖTEL (G)**

Familiar Chat
Cercomela familiaris

L 15cm A widespread, uniform brown chat with a *diagnostic rufous outer tail and rump. Tail has a characteristic dark 'T'.* Also shows narrow pale eye-ring and rufous wash on ear coverts. Darker than Tractrac Chat, with a plumper body and more horizontal stance. Invariably flicks its wings after landing. Gives a harsh, scolding 'shek-shek' alarm call and a warbling trill. Common in rocky and mountainous terrain. **GEWONE SPEKVRETER (A) ROSTSCHWANZSCHMÄTZER (G)**

Karoo Chat
Cercomela schlegelii

L 17cm A *large grey chat* with an upright stance. In flight shows all-white outer-tail feathers and *grey (not white) rump*, which differentiates it from female Mountain Wheatear and Tractrac Chat. Its large size also eliminates confusion with the Tractrac Chat. Imm. is buff-spotted above and scaled below. Call is a typical chat-like 'chak-chak'. Found in desert scrub with scattered bushes and is locally common and thinly distributed along the desert edge in the region. Near-endemic to Namibia. **KAROOSPEKVRETER (A) BLEICHSCHMÄTZER (G)**

Tractrac Chat
Cercomela tractrac

L 14–15cm Namib coastal form has a very *upright posture, is almost white, with darker wings and a darker tail,* and is larger than the inland form. Inland form is darker above with a darker head but still shows white rump and sides of the tail. Gives a soft, fast 'tactac' call and a quiet, musical, bubbling song. Near-endemic to Namibia. Occurs on gravel plains and scrub desert and is a common resident in the region. **WOESTYNSPEKVRETER (A) NAMIBSCHMÄTZER (G)**

Ant-eating Chat
Myrmecocichla formicivora

L 17–18cm Easily identified in flight by the *window-like white patches on its wing tips*. Posture is upright. Appears short-tailed and plump. Ranges from dark brown to mottled black. Male is very dark brown; female is a paler brown. Imm. is paler brown like the female and more mottled than the ad. Gives a short, sharp 'peek' or 'piek' call. Associated with open veld; perches on termite mounds to scan its territory. Common resident; near-endemic. **SWARTPIEK (A) TERMITENSCHMÄTZER (G)**

Mountain Wheatear
Oenanthe monticola

L 17–18cm Has unmistakable *black-and-white pied plumage*. Male shows variable plumage but always has a *white rump, white sides to the tail and a white shoulder patch*. Nondescript, greyish-brown female also shows a white shoulder patch. Imm. is similar to female. Gives a clear, thrush-like, whistling song interspersed with harsh chattering. Nervous and flighty. Common resident; inhabits mountainous and rocky terrain.
BERGWAGTER (A) BERGSCHMÄTZER (G)

Capped Wheatear
Oenanthe pileata

L 17cm In ad. *white eyebrow stripe and forehead contrasting with black cap and black collar* are diagnostic. Can run very fast. In flight, white rump and sides of the tail are conspicuous. Imm. has paler head and collar markings. The song is a loud warbling with slurred chattering, given during the hovering display flight, from the ground or from a raised perch. Common resident that frequents open level veld with little grass cover.
HOËVELDSKAAPWAGTER (A) ERDSCHMÄTZER (G)

Herero Chat
Namibornis herero

L 17cm The *black line that runs through the eye contrasts with a clear white eyebrow stripe*. Outer-tail feathers and rump are rust-coloured; faint streaking is visible on the breast at close range. Female duller than male. Imm. resembles female but is more mottled. Usually silent, but gives a melodious warbling song in the br. season. Endemic to Namibia and southern Angola. Found in arid shrub savanna along the desert edge in the boulder-strewn escarpment zone.
HEREROSPEKVRETER (A) NAMIBSCHNÄPPER (G)

M BOYSEN

White-browed Scrub Robin
Cercotrichas leucophrys

L 14–16cm The most common scrub robin of savanna and woodland, easily identified by its *two white wing bars*. *Rump and base of tail rufous; remainder of tail dark brown, with narrow white tips.* C. l. ovamboensis has greatly reduced streaking, mainly on the sides of the rufous-washed breast. Juv. paler above, with buff spots; breast diffusely mottled (not streaked). Characteristic call at dawn and dusk is a whistled 'seeep po go'. Favours areas with grass cover. **GESTREEPTE WIPSTERT (A) WEISSBRAUEN-HECKENSÄNGER (G)**

M. BUOYSEN

Kalahari Scrub Robin
Cercotrichas paena

L 14–16cm Sandy brown, with a pale eyebrow and rufous rump and uppertail. Easily recognised by the conspicuous *white sides to the tail tip, which contrast with the broad black subterminal tail bar.* Imm. is mottled with sooty black and buff. Gives varied, musical, whistled song interspersed with harsher notes. Common resident and inhabits dry thornveld, thicket and tangled growth around waterholes and dry river beds. **KALAHARIWIPSTERT (A) KALAHARIHECKENSÄNGER (G)**

A. FRONEMAN/IMAGES OF AFRICA

Rockrunner *Achaetops pycnopygius*

L 17–20cm Can be identified by its *heavily streaked, dark back, white breast spotted with black at the sides, and bright rufous belly and undertail.* By comparison, the imm. is lightly streaked. Utters a hollow, melodious, warbling 'rooodle-trrooodlee' call. Most often seen scrambling over rocks in dense undergrowth on hillsides in the escarpment zone. Generally in areas of higher rainfall than the Herero Chat. A common endemic of Namibia and southern Angola. **ROTSVOËL (A) KLIPPENSÄNGER (G)**

M. BUOYSEN

Long-billed Crombec
Sylvietta rufescens

L 11cm A small, plump, greyish bird with buffy cinnamon underparts; appears almost tailless. Easily differentiated from other similar warblers by its long, slightly decurved bill. When feeding, gleans insects from branches and leaves and probes crevices with its long bill. Gives a frequently repeated 'tree-trriit' call. Common resident, it occurs in a wide range of habitats, from woodlands to semi-arid scrub; avoids extremely arid regions. **BOSVELDSTOMPSTERT (A) LANGSCHNABEL-SYLVIETTA (G)**

Cape Penduline-Tit
Anthoscopus minutus

L 8cm Has diagnostic *black forehead extending as eye-stripe. Yellowish belly and flanks and speckled throat* are also diagnostic. Imm. has paler yellow underparts than the ad. Distinguished from the eremomelas by its tiny size, short, more conical bill, rotund body and very short tail. Call is a soft 'tseep'. Occurs in scrub, semi-desert and dry thornveld and is thinly distributed in the drier scrub regions of Namibia. **KAAPSE KAPOKVOËL (A) WEISSSTIRN-BEUTELMEIS (G)**

Chestnut-vented Tit-babbler
Sylvia subcaeruleum

L 15cm A grey bird with a longish, *white-tipped tail and a pale eye.* Has extensive black streaking on the throat. Differs from very similar Layard's Tit-babbler in being darker grey and having a diagnostic *chestnut vent.* Imm. lacks black streaking on the throat. Common resident, most often seen as it creeps through thick thorn bush delivering a loud, explosive 'cheruuup-chee-chee' song. Inhabits tree-and-shrub savanna throughout the region. **BOSVELDTJERIKTIK (A) MEISENSÄNGER (G)**

A. FRONEMAN/IMAGES OF AFRICA

A. MANSON/WIKIMEDIA/CC BY SA 2.0

A. FRONEMAN/IMAGES OF AFRICA

Layard's Tit-babbler *Sylvia layardi*

L 14cm Differs from Chestnut-vented Tit-babbler in *being paler and having a white (not chestnut) vent*. Silvery-white eye contrasts with the dark head, and throat streaking is less pronounced than in Chestnut-vented Tit-babbler. Imm. lacks any streaking on the throat. Gives a clear 'pee-pee-cheeri-cheeri' call. Uncommon and thinly distributed in Namibia. May be found in rocky, hilly areas in thornveld and in desert scrub along dry watercourses. **GRYSTJERIKTIK (A) LAYARDS MEISENSÄNGER (G)**

M. BOOYSEN

Willow Warbler *Phylloscopus trochilus*

L 11cm Small, *yellowish-olive warbler, with yellow underparts and a thin, weak bill*. Distinct yellow on the underparts is restricted to the throat and breast; belly is mainly dull white. Imm. has much brighter yellow eyebrow stripe and face. Gives a short melodious song, descending in scale. A common summer visitor that occurs in a wide range of habitats, from dry thornveld to broadleaved woodland. **HOFSANGER (A) FITIS (G)**

Lesser Swamp Warbler
Acrocephalus gracilirostis

L 14–16cm Although similar to other drab warblers in the region, it is fairly large, with *brownish upperparts and a clearer white throat and breast*. It has a *long, heavy bill, a white eyebrow stripe and dark brown legs*. Imm. resembles the ad. Gives a liquid melodious 'cheerup-chee-trrrree' call. Common resident in Namibia. Often seen low down in reedbeds close to water. **KAAPSE RIETSANGER (A) KAPROHRSÄNGER (G)**

African Reed Warbler
Acrocephalus baeticatus

L 12–13cm A small, obscure warbler with *brown upperparts, off-white underparts and warm, buffy flanks.* Also has a pale eyebrow stripe and dark legs. When compared with similar-looking warblers it is not easy to identify, but it is the most common inhabitant of reedbeds in Namibia. Call is a harsh 'tchak' and the song a jumbled mixture of harsh grating notes and melodious whistles; is also known to mimic phrases of other birds. **KLEINRIETSANGER (A) GARTENROHRSÄNGER (G)**

Desert Cisticola
Cisticola aridulus

L 10cm Like other cisticolas it is notoriously difficult to identify, unless observed calling or displaying. It is tiny, with a *finely streaked forehead and well-marked, buffy back.* Sexes are alike, except that the female has a shorter tail. Imm. is slightly paler below than the ad. Gives a 'zink zink zink' song during its low-level display flight. Common resident that inhabits grasslands in dry areas. **WOESTYNKLOPKLOPPIE (A) KALAHARI-ZISTENSÄNGER (G)**

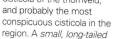

Rattling Cisticola
Cisticola chiniana

L 15cm The most abundant cisticola of the thornveld, and probably the most conspicuous cisticola in the region. A *small, long-tailed bird with a chestnut cap;* often perches openly on the tops of bushes. Imm. is yellower than the ad. When proclaiming its territory from an exposed perch it utters a 'churee-churee' song that ends in a diagnostic, rattling 'cherrrr'. In alarm, gives a repeated scolding 'cheee-cheee' note. Common resident of woodland, savanna and scrub in Namibia. **BOSVELDTINKTINKIE (A) ROTSCHEITEL-ZISTENSÄNGER (G)**

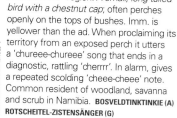

A. FRONEMAN/IMAGES OF AFRICA

Chirping Cisticola   *Cisticola pipiens*

L 14cm The *least strikingly marked of the wetland cisticolas. Br. male distinguished from Luapula Cisticola by its* song, duller rufous cap, pale (not rich rufous) wing panel and more creamy-buff underparts. Call comprises two or three sharp, loud notes followed by a buzzy trill. Locally common in reedbeds and papyrus swamps of Kavango and Zambezi regions. **PIEPENDE TINKTINKIE (A) SUMPFZISTENSÄNGER (G)**

Luapula Cisticola   *Cisticola luapula*

L 14cm Differs from similar Chirping Cisticola by its *richer rufous crown and wing panel, more boldly marked back, greyer tail and paler underparts.* Call is a two-noted 'tic tic' followed by 'wee wee', sometimes given in display flight. Locally common in *Phragmites* reedbeds in permanent wetlands of northern Namibia. **LUAPULATINKTINKIE (G) LUAPULAZISTENSÄNGER**

Grey-backed Cisticola
Cisticola subruficapilla

L 12cm A *long-tailed cisticola with a chestnut cap and a grey back finely streaked with black.* Imm. is duller than the ad. Conspicuous during the br. season when it engages in aerial display. A muffled 'prrrttt' followed by a sharp 'phweee-phwee-phwee' are given in low, fluttery flight over its territory. An uncommon, thinly distributed resident, it is found in scrub areas, on grassy hillsides and on grassy dunes. **GRYSRUGTINKTINKIE (A) BERGZISTENSÄNGER (G)**

Zitting Cisticola
Cisticola juncidis

L 10 cm *Small, short-tailed cisticola.* May be confused with similar Desert Cisticola but is *darker overall and warmer brown* in both br. and non br. plumages. Also shows a rufous, not greyish rump, and tail is darker with more obvious white tip. Obvious undulating display flight, 20–30m high over grassland, uttering a repeated 'zit, zit, zit'. Alarm call is a fast 'chik chik', often repeated. Favours more moist areas than Desert Cisticola. Fairly common resident in the more northerly regions, avoiding dry desert habitat. **LANDERYKLOPKLOPPIE (A) ZISTENSÄNGER (G)**

Black-chested Prinia
Prinia flavicans

L 14cm Unlikely to be confused with other prinias when in br. plumage, it is the only prinia in the region with a *broad black breast band* (usually absent in non-br. plumage). Female has narrower breast band than male. Like other prinias, it has a long tail that is often held cocked at right angles. Imm. lacks the black breast band and is very yellow below. Gives a series of loud 'zzzrt-zzzrt-zzzrt-zzzrt' notes. Common resident; generally frequents arid scrub and thornveld. **SWARTBANDLANGSTERTJIE (A) BRUSTBANDPRINIE (G)**

Rufous-eared Warbler
Malcorus pectoralis

L 15cm Prinia-like habits and appearance. When foraging freely on the ground could be mistaken for a rodent as it scuttles from bush to bush. *Reddish ear coverts and narrow black breast band* are diagnostic. Male has a broader breast band than female. Imm. resembles ad. but lacks distinctive breast band. Gives harsh, scolding 'chweeo, chweeo, chweeo' call. Common resident, occurring in low, stunted karoo scrub, favouring seasonal watercourses. **ROOIOORLANGSTERTJIE (A) ROTBACKENSÄNGER (G)**

Barred Wren-Warbler
Calamonastes fasciolatus

L 14cm A medium-sized warbler with *barring from chin to belly and brown eyes and legs.* Often holds its long tail cocked or fanned over its back. Br. male has a plain brown throat and breast. Imm. more rufous than ad. and shows a yellowish wash on the breast. An inconspicuous bird, it is best located by its call: a thin 'trrreee' and a repeated 'pleelip-pleelip'. Common resident, occurring in dry thornveld and broadleaved woodland. **GEBANDE SANGER (A) BINDENSÄNGER (G)**

M. BOOYSEN

Grey-backed Camaroptera
Camaroptera brevicaudata

L 12cm Recognised by its *off-white to greyish underparts, olive green upperparts and greyish nape and mantle.* Imm. lightly streaked below. Keeps a low profile in thick vegetation and habitually cocks its tail. When excited or disturbed, emits a metallic clicking sound, but its normal calls include a loud, snapping 'bidup-bidup-bidup' and a nasal 'neeeehh'. Common resident. Occurs in thornveld and thickets in broadleaved woodland and scrub. **GRYSRUGKWÊKWÊVOËL (A) GRAURÜCKEN-GRASMÜCKE (G)**

A. FRONEMAN/IMAGES OF AFRICA

Yellow-breasted Apalis
Apalis flavida

L 12cm Identified by its diagnostic *grey head, white throat, yellow breast and white belly.* Male is further distinguished by a small black bar on the lower breast. Imm. is paler yellow on the breast. Call is a rapid buzzy 'chizzick-chizzick-chizzick'. Like other apalises it is always on the move in the forest or bush. Favours the lower or mid-stratum of the canopy. Common resident of broadleaved woodland in northeastern Namibia. **GEELBORSKLEINJANTJIE (A) GELBBRUST-FEINSÄNGER (G)**

♂

♀

A. FRONEMAN/IMAGES OF AFRICA (TOP)

Chat Flycatcher *Bradornis infuscatus*

L 20cm *Uniform brownish above, with paler underparts. A pale brown panel on the folded secondaries* helps to identify this large chat of thrush-like proportions. Imm. is heavily spotted with buff above and below. Gives a rich, warbled 'cher-cher-cherrip' song, interspersed with squeaky, hissing notes. Common but unevenly distributed resident. Occurs in pairs in desert scrub and stunted thornveld. **GROOTVLIEËVANGER (A) DROSSELSCHNÄPPER (G)**

Marico Flycatcher
Bradornis mariquensis

L 18cm A nondescript flycatcher. *Uniform buffish-brown upperparts contrast with clear white underparts.* Imm. is heavily spotted with buff above and streaked with brown below. The song is a soft 'tsii-cheruk-tukk'. Perches conspicuously along roadsides hawking insects and often returns to the same perch. Common resident. Found in mixed thornveld and open dry broadleaved woodland. **MARICOVLIEËVANGER (A) MARICOSCHNÄPPER (G)**

Spotted Flycatcher
Muscicapa striata

L 13–14cm Told apart from the larger, pale-breasted Marico Flycatcher by its *streaked and spotted breast and forehead.* Imm. is mottled brown and buff, but is unlikely to be seen in the region. A common summer visitor and mostly silent in Namibia, but occasionally utters a soft 'tzee'. Has very upright posture when perched and frequently flicks its wings on alighting or when agitated. Usually returns to the same perch after a sortie for flying insects. Frequents a wide range of habitats. **EUROPESE VLIEËVANGER (A) GRAUSCHNÄPPER (G)**

African Paradise Flycatcher
Terpsiphone viridis

L 17cm (br. male up to 34cm) *Dark head and breast, bright blue bill and eye-ring, and chestnut back and tail.* Br. male has very long tail. Female and imm. have short tails and imm. is duller. Noisy and active, rarely settling for long. Harsh 'tic-tic-chaa-chaa' notes are often heard before the bird is seen. Song is a loud 'twee-tiddly-te-te'. A common summer br. visitor in the north, in moist riverine and broadleaved woodland and suburban gardens. **PARADYSVLIEËVANGER (A) PARADIESSCHNÄPPER (G)**

A. FRONEMAN/IMAGES OF AFRICA (BOTH)

♂   ♀

Chinspot Batis
Batis molitor

L 12–13cm A widespread batis of woodland in Namibia. Female has a *diagnostic chestnut throat spot and neat breast band; wing bar is white.* Male very similar to male Pririt Batis but has *white (not dark mottled) flanks.* Juv. resembles female, but head and breast are mottled brown. Call is 2–4 clear descending whistles 'teuu-teuu-teuu' ('three blind mice') and harsh 'chrr-chrr' notes. Common in broadleaved woodland of northeastern Namibia. **WITLIESBOSBONTROKKIE (A) WEISSFLANKENSCHNÄPPER (G)**

Pririt Batis
Batis pririt

L 12cm A *small black-and-white flycatcher.* Female has a distinctive chestnut wash over the throat and breast. Male differs in having a broad black breast band. Both sexes have indistinct black markings on the flank. Imm. resembles female. Call is a series of slow 'teuu, teuu, teuu, teuu' notes, descending in scale. Common near-endemic resident of acacia thorn tree-and-shrub savanna. Absent from moist teak woodland in northeastern Namibia. **PRIRITBOSBONTROKKIE (A) PRIRITSCHNÄPPER (G)**

♂

M. BOOYSEN (INSET)

♀

White-tailed Shrike
Lanioturdus torquatus

L 15cm Striking, with diagnostic *contrasting black, white and grey plumage, long legs and very short tail.* Characteristic upright stance makes it appear almost tailless. Imm. similar to ad. but has a mottled crown. Sexes alike. The call consists of a series of clear, drawn-out whistles and harsh cackling. Common endemic of Namibia; most commonly seen on the ground or scrambling over rocks on hillsides in the thornveld and shrub savanna of the central and northwestern escarpment zone.
KORTSTERTLAKSMAN (A) DROSSELWÜRGER (G)

Orange River White-eye
Zosterops pallidus

L 11cm Warbler-like; *buffy-yellow on the flanks and olive/grey above. Ring of white feathers around the eye is diagnostic.* Imm. duller than the ad. In moving bird parties, pairs keep in contact by giving continual soft, sweet 'tweee-tuuu-twee-twee' calls. Commonly found in groups in a wide range of habitats, including suburban gardens. Common resident of Namibia. **GARIEPGLASOGIE (A) ORANJEBRILLENVOGEL (G)**

M BOOYSEN

African Yellow White-eye
Zosterops senegalensis

L 10–12cm *Bright yellow; lacks any green tones in underparts and has yellower upperparts than* Orange River White-eye. Juv. duller than ad., with greener upperparts. Call is a loud, melodious, whistled 'tweee-tuuu-twee-twee'. Groups make continuous twittering contact calls. Common resident of woodlands, shrub, forests and gardens in northeastern Namibia. **GEELGLASOGIE (A) SENEGALBRILLENVOGEL (G)**

Cape Wagtail
Motacilla capensis

L 20cm Derives its name from its habit of continually moving its tail up and down when walking or at rest. The unmarked, *greyish-brown upperparts combined with a narrow black breast band* are diagnostic. Imm. is duller than ad., with a buff-yellow wash over the belly. Call is a clear, ringing 'tseee-chee-chee' and a whistled, trilling song. Uncommon and thinly distributed. Favours damp and marshy areas and is also found in city parks and gardens.
GEWONE KWIKKIE (A) KAPSTELZE (G)

African Pipit
Anthus cinnamomeus

L 17cm Fairly nondescript, with *buff-and-brown plumage and streaking on the breast*. In flight, prominent *white outer-tail feathers* are visible. Imm. is darker above and more heavily streaked than ad. Gives a 'trrit-trrit-trrit' song during display and utters a 'chisseet' alarm call when flushed. Feeds on the ground, running short distances before stopping to pick up food. Most likely to be seen in the open veld or grasslands. Common but thinly distributed in the region.
GEWONE KOESTER (A) WEIDELANDPIEPER (G)

juv.

Magpie Shrike
Corvinella melanoleuca

L 40–50cm (incl. tail) A large, *very long-tailed black shrike with white scapular bars, white tips to flight feathers and a whitish rump*. Female has whitish flanks; tail averages slightly shorter. Juv. is dull sooty-brown, with buff tips to underpart feathers. Call is a liquid, whistled 'pee-leeo' or 'pur-leeoo'; also gives a scolding 'tzeeaa' alarm call. Common resident of savanna and open woodland, favouring acacias. Usually in groups of 4–12 birds.
LANGSTERTLAKSMAN (A) ELSTERWÜRGER (G)

M. BOOYSEN

transitional

Southern White-crowned Shrike
Eurocephalus anguitimens

L 23–25cm A large, robust shrike. Easy to identify as it is the only shrike in the region to show a *white crown and white forehead*. Throat and breast are also white; belly and flanks are washed with buff. Imm. is paler than ad., with a mottled brown body. Gives a shrill whistling 'kree, kree, kree' and harsh chattering and bleating calls. Gregarious. Common resident of Namibia; frequents thornveld and dry woodland. **KREMETARTLAKSMAN (A) WEISSSCHEITELWÜRGER (G)**

Red-backed Shrike
Lanius collurio

L 18cm Smallish, compact, with *chestnut back and wings* and a fairly short tail (blackish with white base to outer tail). Male has *black face mask, grey crown, nape and rump and plain pinkish underparts*. Female is duller, with grey-brown mask, grey wash on head and rump, and brown chevrons on flanks. Lacks white scapular bar of juv. Common Fiscal. Imm. is like female, with upperparts finely barred darker brown. Gives warbled song before northern migration. Common, solitary. Palearctic migrant in savanna and open woodland. **ROOIRUGLAKSMAN (A) NEUNTÖTER (G)**

Lesser Grey Shrike
Lanius minor

L 20–22cm *White underparts contrast with the grey back and extensive black mask, which encompasses the forehead.* Female is duller, often with less black on the forehead. Imm. has buffy underparts with light barring. The soft 'chuk' and warbled song are rarely heard. A common summer visitor. Obvious along roadsides, where it perches on telephone wires and atop bushes and poles. Frequents mixed dry thornveld and semi-desert scrub. **GRYSLAKSMAN (A) SCHWARZSTIRNWÜRGER (G)**

A. FRONEMAN/IMAGES OF AFRICA (MAIN IMAGE)

A. FRONEMAN/IMAGES OF AFRICA

Common Fiscal
Lanius collaris

L 21–23cm Has *black upperparts, white underparts, prominent white eye-stripe and prominent white shoulder patches*. Female has rufous flank patch. Imm. is greyish-brown with grey barring on underparts. Other black-and-white shrikes are furtive, but this conspicuous bird hunts from exposed perches. Song is harsh, melodious and jumbled, with mimicry of other birds. Common resident in a range of habitats but avoids dense woodland. **FISKAALLAKSMAN (A) FISKALWÜRGER (G)**

imm.

P. RYAN

White-crested Helmetshrike
Prionops plumatus

L 19–20cm In flight shows pied plumage with white flashes in the wings and white outer-tail feathers. At rest, *clear white underparts, grey crown, white collar, yellow eye-ring and black ear coverts* are visible. Imm. is duller than ad. and lacks yellow eye-ring and black ear coverts. Call consists of a jumble of chattering and whistling. Common resident. Gregarious; small groups flit through mixed woodland and thornveld. **WITHELMLAKSMAN (A) BRILLENWÜRGER (G)**

Brubru
Nilaus afer

L 14cm Could be mistaken for a batis, but its large size and thick bill obviate confusion. *Black-and-white chequered back, broad white eyebrow stripe and russet flank stripe* are diagnostic features. Female is duller than the male. Imm. has brown-and-white mottling below. Gives a soft, trilling 'prrrr, prrrr' call and a piercing, whistled 'tioooo'. Common resident in open tree-and-shrub savanna throughout Namibia, avoiding more arid areas. **BONTROKLAKSMAN (A) BRUBRU (G)**

A. FRONEMAN/IMAGES OF AFRICA

Black-backed Puffback
Dryoscopus cubla

L 16–18cm The only puffback presently known from Namibia. *Male is boldly marked black and white.* Female and juv. are duller, often with buffy wash, but always have diagnostic pale supercilium. Juv. has brown eyes. Call is a sharp repeated 'chick, weeo'; male utters loud 'chok chok chok' in flight. Common in woodland, thickets and forest canopy.
SNEEUBAL (A) SCHNEEBALLWÜRGER (G)

Swamp Boubou
Laniarius bicolor

L 23cm Identified by its *black upperparts with a white wing stripe and clear all-white underparts (with no trace of rufous or pink coloration).* Imm. is spotted with buff above and barred below. Call is diagnostic, a clear ringing 'hoouu', often in duet, followed by harsher 'kik-kik-kik' sounds. A skulking inhabitant of thick tangles along rivers and in reedbeds; common on the northern river systems of Namibia. **MOERASWATERFISKAAL (A) ZWEIFARBENWÜRGER (G)**

M BOOYSEN

Crimson-breasted Shrike
Laniarius atrococcineus

L 25cm Among the most strikingly coloured bushveld birds. *Bright crimson underparts and black upperparts, offset by a white flash down the wing* make it unmistakable. Imm. is barred with greyish-brown, showing varying amounts of crimson below. Gives an unusual clonking call and a harsh 'trrrrr'. Common resident, though not always easily seen as it tends to skulk in the undergrowth of thornveld and dry rivercourses.
ROOIBORSLAKSMAN (A) ROTBAUCHWÜRGER (G)

Brown-crowned Tchagra
Tchagra australis

L 18–19cm Shrike-like, with *russet wings and a white-tipped tail*. Other identifying features include an obvious *black eye-stripe and a white eyebrow stripe*. Imm. is duller version of the ad. Tends to skulk in thick tangles and undergrowth in thornveld. More conspicuous in br. season: flutters in display flight, then descends slowly, giving its 'weee-chee-chee-chee' song. Common Namibian resident. Frequents bushveld and forested areas of the region.

ROOIVLERKTJAGRA (A) DAMARATSCHAGRA (G)

DEAN CHALMERS

Bokmakierie   *Telophorus zeylonus*

L 23cm *Bluish-grey head, bright lemon yellow underparts and broad black breast band are diagnostic*. In flight, shows a vivid yellow tip to the dark green tail. Imm. lacks the breast band and is greyish-green below. Gives a variety of calls, the most common of which is a 'bok-bok-kik', from which its common name is derived. Uncommon, thinly distributed resident of Namibia. Found in scrub-filled valleys in mountainous areas.

BOKMAKIERIE (A) BOKMAKIRI (G)

Cape Glossy Starling
Lamprotornis nitens

L 25cm A short-tailed starling. From a distance appears to be completely black; at reasonably close proximity *iridescent coloration* is visible. Ear patches, head, belly and flanks are bright, shiny green. The *bright orange eye* is wide and staring. Imm. is duller than ad., with straw-coloured eyes. Gives a slurred 'trrr-chree-chrrrr' song. The most common glossy starling in Namibia; frequents thornveld, mixed woodland and suburbia. **KLEINGLANSSPREEU (A)**
ROTSCHULTER-GLANZSTAR (G)

Meves's Starling *Lamprotornis mevesii*

L 34cm *A medium-sized glossy starling, with a very long graduated tail.* Longer and slimmer than Burchell's Starling, with a much longer tail. Juv. duller, with brownish head and matt black underparts; tail is shorter but still distinctly long and graduated. Gives a querulous, rather harsh 'keeeaaaa' call, higher-pitched than that of Burchell's Starling; also various squawks. Locally common resident in the north, frequenting tall mopane woodland and riverine forests. **LANGSTERTGLANSSPREEU (A) MEVES-GLANZSTAR (G)**

Burchell's Starling
Lamprotornis australis

L 32–34cm The *largest starling in Namibia.* Glossy; with *long, wedge-shaped tail and rounded wings;* the flight is noticeably laboured and floppy. Imm. duller than the ad. Gives a rough, throaty series of chuckles and chortles. Regularly seen along roadsides, where it flies up lazily from verges into trees or onto telephone wires. Common resident of thornveld and dry broadleaved woodland. **GROOTGLANSSPREEU (A) RIESENGLANZSTAR (G)**

Violet-backed Starling
Cinnyricinclus leucogaster

L 15–17cm Male readily identified by its stunning *glossy amethyst upperparts, throat and upper breast;* this colour may vary with wear from bluish to coppery. Female and juv. are unique among African starlings in having heavily streaked plumage; more likely to be confused with other passerines. Call is a soft but sharp 'tip, tip'; song is short series of buzzy whistles. Found in most tree-and-shrub savanna and woodland. Common resident and intra-African migrant. **WITBORSSPREEU (A) AMETHYSTGLANZSTAR (G)**

A. FRONEMAN/IMAGES OF AFRICA (MAIN IMAGE)

Pale-winged Starling
Onychognathus nabouroup

L 27cm A long-tailed starling; in flight, shows a highly visible *white patch* in the primaries from which it derives its name. Has *slightly glossy dark blue-black plumage and a bright orange eye.* Imm. duller than the ad. Call is a ringing 'preeeooo' given in flight, as well as warbling calls like those of the Cape Glossy Starling. Inhabits rocky ravines and cliffs in dry and desert regions but has also colonised cities and towns. Common resident of Namibia.
BLEEKVLERKSPREEU (A) BERGSTAR (G)

Wattled Starling *Creatophora cinerea*

L 21cm Greyish starling with black-pointed wings and a short black tail. Br. male is very conspicuous with *black-and-yellow head and black wattles.* Female has a whitish rump; imm. is brownish-grey, with whitish rump. Gives a sharp 'ssreeeeo' call. Nomadic and abundant when br. Found in large flocks in open scrub areas, light woodland and grassland. **LELSPREEU (A) LAPPENSTAR (G)**

non-br.

br.

A. FRONEMAN/IMAGES OF AFRICA (BOTTOM IMAGE)

Scarlet-chested Sunbird
Chalcomitra senegalensis

L 14cm Large, chunky sunbird. Male's *black body and scarlet chest* are unmistakable. At close range, iridescent blue flecks are visible on male's breast. Female is greyish-olive above and very heavily mottled below. Imm. resembles female. Song is a loud whistled 'cheeup-chup-toop-toop-toop' call. Male is bold and conspicuous, chasing other birds from his territory. Common resident, found in mixed dry and moist woodland, thornveld and in suburbia. **ROOIBORSSUIKERBEKKIE (A)**
ROTBRUST-GLANZKÖPFCHEN (G)

N. DENNIS/IMAGES OF AFRICA (BOTH)

♂ ♀

Marico Sunbird *Cinnyris mariquensis*

L 12cm Male has a *scarlet chest band and iridescent purple breast band contrasting with the black belly. Head and back are metallic greenish-blue; bill is long and decurved.* Female has drab olive-brown upperparts and pale yellow, streaked underparts. Female's distinguishing feature is a long, robust, decurved bill. Imm. resembles female. Gives a typically chippering sunbird call. Common resident; frequents thornveld and dry broadleaved woodland. **MARICOSUIKERBEKKIE (A) BINDENNEKTARVOGEL (G)**

Dusky Sunbird *Cinnyris fusca*

L 10cm *Black head, throat and back and contrasting white belly* are usually diagnostic in the male; sometimes has only a *black line running from the throat to the breast.* Pectoral tufts in both sexes are orange. Female has light grey-brown upperparts and off-white underparts. Imm. resembles female but has a black throat. Gives short warbling song interspersed with a scolding 'chrrr-chrrr'. Common resident of dry thornveld, dry and wooded rocky valleys and scrub desert in the region. **NAMAKWASUIKERBEKKIE (A) RUSSNEKTARVOGEL (G)**

M. BODYSEN L. RUDMAN (INSET)

Great Sparrow *Passer motitensis*

L 15cm Male has *bright chestnut back and sides of head* and *chestnut (not grey) rump.* Female is told from female Cape sparrow by *pale chestnut eye-stripe, and dark-streaked chestnut mantle.* Imm. similar to female. Gives a liquid 'cheereep, cheereeu' call. Common resident occurring in dry thornveld; not usually associated with human habitation. **GROOTMOSSIE (A) ROTBRAUNER SPERLING (G)**

Cape Sparrow
Passer melanurus

L 15cm Male is distinctive, being the only sparrow in Namibia to have a *bold black-and-white head pattern*. Female has a *chestnut mantle and faint shadow markings of the male's head pattern*. Call consists of a series of musical cheeps. Common Namibian resident. Although it has adapted to human habitation, is frequently found in remote grassland areas. **GEWONE MOSSIE (A) KAPSPERLING (G)**

Southern Grey-headed Sparrow
Passer diffusus

L 15cm A plain sparrow with a warm *brown back, soft grey head and russet mantle*; sexes alike. Call is a rather slow series of chirping 'tchep tchierp tchep' notes; also gives an alarm rattle. Common resident in woodland and other areas with trees; occurs in gardens but generally avoids urban areas. **GRYSKOPMOSSIE (A) GRAUKOPFSPERLING (G)**

A. FRONEMAN/IMAGES OF AFRICA

White-browed Sparrow-weaver
Plocepasser mahali

L 17cm A large, plump, short-tailed weaver, with a distinctive *broad white eyebrow stripe, conspicuous white rump and white wing stripe*. Male has a black bill; female's bill is horn-coloured. Imm. similar to the ad. but has pinkish-brown bill. Build scruffy nests from dry grass in the outer branches of a tree. A loud liquid 'cheeoop-preeoo-chop' call is given from the colony; also gives a harsher 'chik-chik' alarm call. Common resident, found in thornveld and along dry scrubby rivercourses. **KORINGVOËL (A) MAHALIWEBER (G)**

Sociable Weaver   *Philetairus socius*

L 14cm The *black chin, black-barred flanks and scaly-patterned back* render it unmistakable. Imm. lacks black face mask. In flight, gives a chattering 'chicker-chick-er' call. Gregarious, building enormous communal nests that resemble small haystacks and appear to 'thatch' trees in which they are built. Small flocks are found roaming areas of dry thornveld and tree-lined watercourses in Kalahari sandveld. Usually a common resident in Namibia but becomes nomadic in drought years. **VERSAMELVOËL (A) SIEDELWEBER (G)**

Red-billed Buffalo Weaver
Bubalornis niger

L 22–24cm The only large, black, sparrow-like bird in the region. *Robust red bill, black plumage and white wing patches* are diagnostic. Female and imm. are brown versions of the male. Gives a 'chip-chip-doodley-doodley-doo' song. Breeds communally, making a large untidy nest from bundles of thorny sticks in trees or on electricity pylons. Common resident throughout central and northern Namibia, avoiding the arid desert areas. **BUFFELWEWER (A) BÜFFELWEBER (G)**

Southern Masked Weaver
Ploceus velatus

L 15–16cm Br. male is easily confused with Lesser Masked Weaver but differs in having *brownish-pink legs, a red eye and a black mask that does not extend behind the eye on top of the head and that forms a point on the throat.* Female, non-br. male and imm. are alike, having yellowish underparts and olive-brown upperparts. Call consists of typical swizzling weaver notes. Common resident; breeds in trees overhanging water in thornveld and in suburbia. **SWARTKEELGEELVINK (A) MASKENWEBER (G)**

Lesser Masked Weaver
Ploceus intermedius

L 15cm Slightly smaller than Southern Masked Weaver. Br. male identified by the *shape of its mask, which extends well onto the crown and comes to a rounded (not pointed) end on the throat.* Shows a white eye and blue legs. Imm. and female lack the mask and are yellow below. Call is a typical weaver 'chuk'. Frequents savanna and woodland, breeding colonially in trees overhanging water but also away from water; less common than Southern Masked Weaver. **KLEINGEELVINK (A) CABANISWEBER (G)**

Red-headed Weaver
Anaplectes melanotis

L 14cm A *grey-backed weaver with yellow-edged wing feathers and a long, slender orange-red bill;* belly white. Br. male has a *scarlet head and breast;* lemon yellow in female and non-br. male. Gives high-pitched swizzling song and squeaky 'cherra-cherra' calls. Locally common in moist woodland and gardens of northeastern Namibia. Usually monogamous. **ROOIKOPWEWER (A) SCHARLACHWEBER (G)**

A. FRONEMAN/IMAGES OF AFRICA (BOTH)

Chestnut Weaver *Ploceus rubiginosus*

L 15cm Br. male has *black head and chestnut back and underparts.* Female and non-br. male are dull grey-brown with a yellowish throat ending in a brownish breast band. Imm. similar to the female but has streaking on the breast. Utters the usual 'chuk, chuk' and swizzling weaver-type notes. Occurs nomadically in dry thornveld savanna of central and northern Namibia, in years of good rain. Has become resident in suburban gardens of central Namibia. **BRUINWEWER (A) ROTBRAUNER WEBER (G)**

Red-billed Quelea   *Quelea quelea*

L 12cm Br. male easily identified by *black face bordered with pinkish-red, bright red bill and red legs.* Non-br. male and female are drab but retain the *red bill and legs.* Female in br. plumage shows a horn-coloured bill. Imm. resembles female but has yellowish-pink bill. Song is a mixture of harsh and melodious notes. Concentrates in flocks numbering hundreds or thousands. Common to abundant resident; occurs in dry mixed woodlands and savanna and on farmlands. **ROOIBEKKWELEA (A) BLUTSCHNABELWEBER (G)**

Yellow-crowned Bishop
Euplectes afer

L 10cm Br. male easily identified by striking *black-and-yellow plumage.* Non-br. male and female most closely resemble Southern Red Bishop but are noticeably smaller, more compact and paler, with reduced streaking on the breast and flanks and a prominent yellow eye-stripe. Imm. resembles female. Call consists of a series of buzzing and chirping notes. Found in reedbeds and grasses near water, as well as on agricultural fields and grasslands. Common resident in the north of Namibia. **GOUDGEELVINK (A) TAHAWEBER (G)**

Southern Red Bishop   *Euplectes orix*

L 12cm Br. male distinctive, with contrasting *bright orange-and-black plumage and black forehead and crown.* Female and non-br. male brown and buff, with dark streaking on the underparts. Imm. resembles female. Gives a 'cheet-cheet' flight call. In display flight, male fluffs out his feathers and, with rapid wing beats, whizzes to and fro like a bumble-bee, giving a buzzing, chirping song. A widespread, common resident. Associated with water and occurs in reedbeds adjoining freshwater and agricultural lands. **ROOIVINK (A) ORYXWEBER (G)**

Shaft-tailed Whydah *Vidua regia*

L 12cm (plus 22cm tail in br. male) Br. male is easily identified by *buff-and-black plumage and diagnostic spatulate tips to the elongated tail feathers*. Non-br. male and female slightly paler, with streaked head markings. Imm. dull brown with dark streaking on the back. Displaying males utter a harsh 'tseet-tseet-tseet' call. Common resident, occurring in grassy areas in dry thornveld, but generally absent from broadleaved woodland.
PYLSTERTROOIBEKKIE (A) KÖNIGSWITWE (G)

Long-tailed Paradise Whydah
Vidua paradisaea

L 15cm (plus 23cm tail in br. male) Br. male has a *long tail of stiff downward-curving feathers, tapering to a point. Has black upperparts, black head, yellow hind collar, yellow belly and chestnut breast*. Non-br. male, female and imm. have black bill, off-white head with black stripes and grey-brown upperparts. Call is a sharp 'chip-chip' and a short 'cheroop-cherrup'. Common resident of Namibia; occurs in mixed woodland, especially thornveld.
GEWONE PARADYSVINK (A) SPITZSCHWANZ-PARADIESWITWE (G)

Red-headed Finch
Amadina erythrocephala

L 14cm A small finch, with a *bright red head contrasting with barred and mottled underparts*. Male may be confused with Red-billed Quelea but lacks the black face and has barred (not uniform) underparts. Gives a soft 'zree-zree' flight call and a harsher 'chuk-chuk'. Often seen at Sociable Weaver nests and sometimes forms large flocks when not br. Common resident and occurs in dry woodland, thornveld and scrub. **ROOIKOPVINK (A) ROTKOPFAMADINE (G)**

Scaly-feathered Finch
Sporopipes squamifrons

L 10cm At rest, is an easily identified, tiny finch with *black and white malar stripes, a freckled black-and-white forehead and white-fringed wing and tail feathers.* In flight appears as a grey blur. When flushed, settles on an exposed perch. Imm. lacks malar stripes and freckling on the forehead. Emits an indistinct 'chizz-chizz' call note in flight. Common resident; found in dry thornveld and around cattle enclosures, watering troughs and farm buildings.
BAARDMANNETJIE (A) SCHNURRBÄRTCHEN (G)

Blue Waxbill   *Uraeginthus angolensis*

L 12cm *Powder blue face, breast and tail* make it unmistakable. Female is paler than male, with less blue on the face and underparts; imm. is paler than female. Call is a soft 'kway-kway-sree-seee-seee-seee'. Common resident; usually occurs in pairs or flocks in dry areas of mixed woodland and thornveld. Tame and confiding around human habitation. **GEWONE BLOUSYSIE (A) ANGOLA-SCHMETTERLINGSFINK (G)**

Violet-eared Waxbill
Granatina granatina

L 13cm Male is the most colourful of all southern African waxbills and has *cinnamon body, iridescent violet ear patches, brilliant blue rump, red eyes and red bill.* Biscuit-coloured female is identified by diagnostic violet ear patches and blue rump. Imm. resembles female but lacks violet on the head. Gives a soft whistled 'tiu-woowee' call. Common resident that occurs in woodland and savanna, especially in dry thornveld, on rivercourses, on grassy roadsides and in suburban gardens.
KONINGBLOUSYSIE (A) GRANATASTRILD (G)

A. FRONEMAN/IMAGES OF AFRICA

Common Waxbill
Estrilda astrild

L 11cm A long-tailed waxbill. Sexes are similar, with *bright red bill and face patch and a small reddish patch on the belly*. Imm. is duller version of the ad., with a black bill. Gives a nasal 'cher-cher-cher' call and a 'ping-ping' flight note. Common resident. Found in long grass in damp areas alongside rivers and in reedbeds.
ROOIBEKSYSIE (A) WELLENASTRILD (G)

Black-faced Waxbill
Estrilda erythronotos

L 12cm Easily identified by its *greyish-brown body and head, conspicuous black face patch and dark red rump and flanks*. Imm. and female are duller versions of the male. Call is a high-pitched 'chuloweee'. Common resident of Namibia, occurring in thick tangles in dry thornveld and grassy areas and in suburban gardens.
SWARTWANGSYSIE (A) ELFENASTRILD (G)

A. FRONEMAN/IMAGES OF AFRICA

Green-winged Pytilia
Pytilia melba

L 13cm A brightly coloured finch, showing a *crimson face, bill and throat, blue-grey nape, and boldly barred belly and flanks*. Female has all-grey head and breast. Imm. similar to female but is more olive above and plain greyish below. Gives a pretty, trilling song that rises and falls in pitch. Also known to utter a short 'wick' call. Common resident in the region and frequents dry woodland and thornveld and suburban gardens. **GEWONE MELBA (A) BUNTASTRILD (G)**

♂

A. FRONEMAN/IMAGES OF AFRICA (BOTH)

♀

White-throated Canary
Crithagra albogularis

L 16cm *A large pale grey-brown canary with a heavy bill, white throat, small white supercilium and diagnostic greenish-yellow rump.* Larger than female Yellow Canary, with a much larger bill and unstreaked breast. Juv. lightly streaked above and on breast. Song is a rich jumbled mix of melodious notes; contact call is a querulous 'tsuu-eeeee'. Near-endemic. Common resident and local nomad in coastal thicket and semi-desert.
WITKEELKANARIE (A) WEISSKEHLGIRLITZ (G)

Black-throated Canary
Crithagra atrogularis

L 11cm A small, nondescript pale grey canary, heavily streaked with dark brown on the upperparts. Has a diagnostic *black-speckled throat and bright yellow rump.* Female has less black on throat. Imm. is spotted on throat. Gives a prolonged series of wheezy whistles and chirrups. The most common small canary seen in most parts of Namibia. Occurs near waterholes in dry broadleaved woodland and thornveld.
BERGKANARIE (A) ANGOLAGIRLITZ (G)

Yellow Canary   *Crithagra flaviventris*

L 13cm The brightest yellow canary found in Namibia. In bright sunlight, male appears *bright golden-yellow all over*; much more yellow than any weaver. Female and imm. are drabber, *greyish-green with streaked upper- and underparts.* Call is a fast, jumbled series of 'chissick' and 'cheeree' notes. Common resident that occurs from desert-edge scrub to thornveld, and in well-wooded dry river beds.
GEELKANARIE (A) GELBBAUCHGIRLITZ (G)

Lark-like Bunting *Emberiza impetuani*

L 14cm *Lack of diagnostic field characters in this drab bird* are clues to its identification. Might be mistaken for a lark but displays bunting-like behaviour, hopping over stones and foraging around for seeds on bare ground. Imm. is paler than ad. Contact call is a short 'tuc-tuc'. Occurs in dry areas on open plains, on the desert edge and in rocky valleys. Nomadic, being very common in some areas and then vanishing for long periods.

VAALSTREEPKOPPIE (A) LERCHENAMMER (G)

Cinnamon-breasted Bunting
Emberiza tahapisi

L 14cm Can be identified by its *black throat, black-and-white head and diagnostic cinnamon underparts*. In female and imm., which both show the diagnostic cinnamon underparts, black-and-white head markings are less bold. Gives a grating rattled song and a soft 'pee-pee-wee' call. Common resident; nomadic when not br. and frequents rocky slopes in mountainous terrain and mixed woodland. **KLIPSTREEPKOPPIE (A) BERGAMMER (G)**

P. RYAN (BOTTOM), A. FRONEMAN/IMAGES OF AFRICA (TOP)

Golden-breasted Bunting
Emberiza flaviventris

L 15cm *Yellow-orange breast, chestnut mantle and black-and-white-striped head* are diagnostic. White wing bars are conspicuous in flight. Female and imm. are duller versions of male. Often reveals its presence by giving a nasal buzzy 'zzhrrr' call or singing its varied 'weechee-weechee-weechee' song from within the canopy of a tree. A common Namibian resident found in thornveld, broadleaved woodland and suburban gardens. **ROOIRUGSTREEPKOPPIE (A) GELBBAUCHAMMER (G)**

RECOMMENDED READING

Cohen, C., Spottiswoode, C. & Rossouw, J. 2006. *Sasol Southern African Birdfinder*. Cape Town: Struik Nature

Mannheimer, C.A. & Curtis, B.A. (eds) 2009. *Le Roux and Muller's Field Guide to the Trees and Shrubs of Namibia*. Windhoek: Macmillan Education Namibia.

Mendelsohn, J., Jarvis, A., Roberts, C. & Robertson, T. 2002. *Atlas of Namibia: A portrait of the land and its people*. Cape Town: David Philip Publishers.

Sinclair, I., Hockey, P. & Tarboton, W. 2011. *Sasol Birds of Southern Africa*. Cape Town: Struik Nature.

INDEX TO SCIENTIFIC NAMES

INDEX TO GERMAN NAMES

INDEX TO AFRIKAANS NAMES

INDEX TO COMMON NAMES